THE **MINI** ROUGH GUIDE TO

ST LUCIA

HOW TO DOWNLOAD YOUR FREE EBOOK

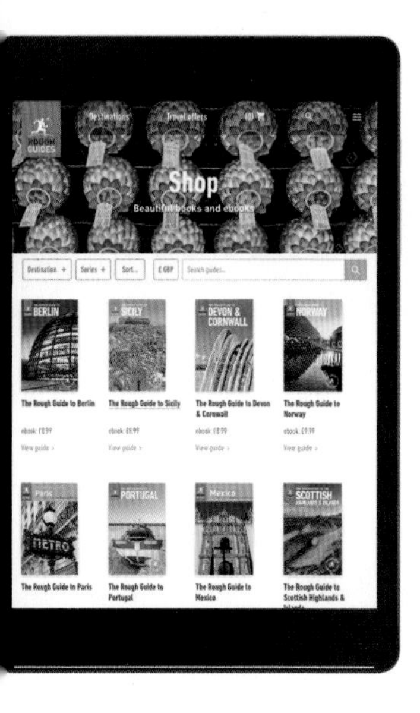

1. Visit **www.roughguides.com/free-ebook** or scan the **QR code** below

2. Enter the code **stlucia923**

3. Follow the simple step-by-step instructions

For troubleshooting contact: mail@roughguides.com

10 THINGS NOT TO MISS

1. **CASTRIES CENTRAL MARKET**
   Vendors sell a huge variety of island produce – including fruit, vegetables, spices and flowers – in and around the old iron building. See page 31.

2. **PIGEON ISLAND NATIONAL LANDMARK**
   Legends abound of pirates and naval exploits; find ruined fortresses and lookouts to explore. See page 39.

3. **GRAND ANSE**
   This huge expanse of sand on the northeast coast is one of the best places for turtle watching. See page 49.

4. **ST LUCIA DISTILLERS**
   The rum distillery showcases traditional and modern methods of producing this iconic Caribbean spirit. See page 53.

5. **ANSE CHASTENET**
   Snorkel or dive to see the colourful reef in the marine reserve. See page 49.

6. **EDMUND FOREST RESERVE**
   Hike and birdwatch with a forest ranger. See page 92.

7. **THE PITONS**
   These iconic twin peaks feature on every postcard. See page 70.

8. **CAP MOULE À CHIQUE**
   Climb to the lighthouse for a panoramic view of the island. See page 76.

9. **MARIA ISLANDS NATURE RESERVE**
   Tiny islands off the southeast coast are home to rare reptiles and nesting migratory birds. See page 77.

10. **DIAMOND BOTANICAL GARDENS, MINERAL BATHS AND WATERFALL**
    History, hikes and glorious herb and flower gardens await. See page 63.

A PERFECT DAY

7.30am

Breakfast. Start the day with a breakfast of saltfish accras — fried fish cakes made from salted cod and mixed spices. Alternatively, feast on fresh mango, papaya and pineapple, accompanied by passionfruit, guava or soursop juice and cocoa tea.

8.30am

Castries. Kick off an island tour with a stop in the capital, calling by the market to pick up edible souvenirs such as cocoa, spices or hot sauces. Wander around the harbour to see the variety of boats and ships and stroll across Derek Walcott Square to the Cathedral.

10.00am

St Lucia Distillers. Sign up for an exuberant, informative "rhythm of rum" tour to learn how the punchy spirit has been made for centuries. It rounds off with a tasting of some 20 different rums to the tune of steel pans.

Noon

Plas Kassav. Drive down the west coast, pausing at family-run *Plas Kassav* to sample some delicious sweet and savoury cassava bread treats. As you continue along this scenic route, photo opportunities emerge around every curve.

1.00pm

Soufrière. Work up an appetite exploring St Lucia's former French capital, then enjoy lunch at one of Soufrière's many restaurants. For local flavours and plenty of veggie options, reserve a table at *Orlando's*, or head to *Boucan* at *Rabot Hotel* for jaw-dropping views of the Pitons and a cacao-centric menu.

IN ST LUCIA

2.00pm

Sulphur springs. Swing by *Zaka Art Café* for top-notch crafts and coffee en route to the bubbling mud and steaming vents of Soufrière's 'drive-in' volcano. Continue down to the south coast, stopping at Choiseul Art Gallery, taking a peek at the fishing village of Laborie, and skirting the airport at Vieux Fort.

4.00pm

Anse de Sables. Stretch your legs with a walk along the sand – or maybe even a dip in the sea – before lingering over a drink at the beach café, where you can admire the view over to the Maria Islands. Then head up the east coast back to Castries.

6.00pm

Sunset cocktails. It's time for a scenic sundowner at *The Coal Pot*, which is also a great place for dinner if you're hungry – think fine French cuisine infused with Caribbean flair, and a wonderful waterside setting.

8.00pm

Dinner. If you've held out for food, Rodney Bay is a top spot for dinner. Wander the strip until you find whatever takes your fancy – from creamy coconut curry, to flame-grilled lobster, the choice is wide.

10.00pm

On the town. Roam Rodney Bay's bars to enjoy plenty of live music. Come Friday, fun-seekers will want to hotfoot it to the Gros Islet Friday Night Jump-up, a lively street party that dances to the beat of reggae, soca and calypso.

CONTENTS

HIGHLIGHTS

A NOTE TO READERS

At Rough Guides, we always strive to bring you the most up-to-date information. This book was produced during a period of continuing uncertainty caused by the Covid-19 pandemic, so please note that content is more subject to change than usual. We recommend checking the latest restrictions and official guidance.

OVERVIEW

Blessed with a bounty of world-class beaches, it's little wonder that the small-but-spectacular Caribbean island of St Lucia (pronounced *Loo-sha*) attracts hundreds of thousands of sun-seekers each year. While most visitors may come expecting an archetypal sea, sun and sand kind of trip, many leave having experienced a whole lot more, for St Lucia offers a wealth of activities — from hiking and zip-lining tropical forests, to exploring some of the region's best reefs along the Caribbean coast. The Atlantic-buffeted side provides excellent windsurfing, while its remote stretches of sand also attract nesting turtles. Meanwhile, St Lucia's interior is lush and green: the golden coastline giving way to wildlife-rich forest

Vigie Beach, Castries

Castries market

reserves in the mountains and on the Pitons, the island's iconic duo of cone-shaped peaks.

LANDSCAPE

Lying at the southern end of the Lesser Antilles chain, St Lucia is part of the Windward Islands group, with Martinique 34km (21 miles) to the north, St Vincent 34km (21 miles) to the south and Barbados 160km (100 miles) to the southeast. The island sprawls across 617 sq km (238 sq miles) of undulating hills and mountains, which are cloaked by native trees, coconut palms, banana plantations and several types of forest. The second-largest of the Windward Islands group – only Dominica is bigger – volcanic St Lucia is 43km (27 miles) long and 22km (14 miles) wide, laced by beaches of charcoal-black or blonde sand and dotted with hot sulphur springs. The rich, fertile soil is ripe for growing the bounty of the island, from fresh fruit to seasonal vegetables.

St Lucia has a tropical, humid climate that provides warm sunshine most of the year, cooled by northeastern trade winds. Showers at any time of year keep the land Kermit-green.

PEOPLE AND HERITAGE

The island population of around 185,000 comprises people of African, Native American, European and East Indian descent. European settlement, indentured labour and slavery account for the island's ethnic mix, with disease, war and colonization contributing to the loss of the island's Native population, which was virtually wiped out by the time enslaved Africans were transported here in the late seventeenth century.

While very few of the island's inhabitants today can trace their ancestry directly to the Kalinago, an Indigenous people who lived on the island at the time of colonization, some St Lucians are of mixed African and Native heritage.

THE KWÉYÒL TONGUE

Kwéyòl began as an oral language that initially helped the French and groups from different parts of the African continent communicate effectively. It was derived from elements of French, a variety of African vocabulary and grammar, English and a little Spanish. While St Lucian Kwéyòl did not have an official written form until the twentieth century, thanks to the efforts of community groups and a rise in published literature, it's increasingly thriving. In 1998 Kwéyòl was officially recognized in the St Lucia House of Assembly and in 1999 the New Testament was published in Kwéyòl, a project that took 15 years to complete, followed in 2001 by a Kwéyòl dictionary for the Ministry of Education. Today Kwéyòl language and culture are celebrated on Jounen Kwéyòl (Creole Day) on the last Sunday of October.

Candy-coloured Choiseul

People with an African heritage are likely to be descendants of enslaved people brought as forced labour to work the land, while St Lucians of European heritage are most likely the descendants of settlers, plantation owners and poor White labourers. There are also descendants of East Indian indentured labourers who arrived after the abolition of slavery. Today, around 80 percent of the population is of African origin, under 3 percent of East Indian extraction, with 12 percent of mixed heritage, and people of European origin making up the remainder. This is a Creole society in its broadest sense: a rich and rare combination of cultures, languages and cuisine.

LANGUAGE AND CULTURE

Although St Lucia has been a British territory since 1814 and the official language is English; French culture pervades. A melodic French Creole (Kwéyòl) is spoken by more than 90 percent of people in informal arenas and, due to a drive to preserve and promote Creole traditions, it's increasingly used in official circles as well. Creole culture and heritage is important and efforts are being made to hold on to the rich folklore, music and language. There are annual festivals, which include traditional storytellers, folk singers and dancers and carnival masqueraders.

The French influence can be seen in place and family names and also in the island's closeness to the neighbouring French *département* of Martinique. There are common linguistic elements within St Lucian and Martinican Creole. However, St Lucian Kwéyòl isn't as close to the French language as one might imagine.

The French influence can also be seen in religion. Over two-thirds of islanders are Roman Catholic and the church plays an important part in the lives of ordinary people. However, living by traditional Christian values hasn't prevented St Lucians from retaining elements of the old West African belief system and folklore – *obeah*, which was decriminalized in St Lucia in 2004. An *obeah* man or woman works spells and creates potions from roots and other forest plants that can heal or harm.

A cocoa pod at Fondoux

Before the advent of modern medicine, the healing practitioner was sought out to cure illnesses, using ancient herbal remedies. Today, people are turning back to nature to recoup knowledge about the medicinal properties of native plants.

Foreign flowers

Flowering trees such as the immortelle or African tulip tree provide bursts of colour but are not native to St Lucia.

ENVIRONMENT AND WILDLIFE

St Lucia has a thriving forest covering 77 sq km (30 sq miles) and considerable biodiversity of flora and fauna. Although a large proportion of native forest was cut down for plantation crops in colonial times, much of the remaining rainforest is now protected to safeguard the island's water supply and wildlife. Fresh water cascades through the mountains, the rivers and streams, feeding the land below.

St Lucia has the distinction of having the highest number of endemic birds in the Eastern Caribbean – the St Lucia parrot, St Lucia Pewee, St Lucia Warbler, St Lucia Oriole, St Lucia Black Finch, and the critically endangered, possibly extinct, Semper's Warbler.

Other notable endemic species include the St Lucia whiptail lizard, and the non-venomous St Lucia racer. With only 18 individuals thought to remain, this is likely to be the world's rarest snake. Also native to the island are the boa constrictor (known locally as the *tete chien*) and the venomous fer-de-lance. Though rarely seen, walkers should be mindful of them along the dry scrub areas of the east coast. Forest trails may also offer sighting of guinea pig-like agoutis and iguanas – a new species of lizard was discovered here in 2020.

St Lucia has worked to preserve the marine environment that attracts visitors and provides livelihoods for fishermen, with diverse marine life found on the coral reefs of the west and south. Low reefs and mangroves also proliferate along the east coast close to the Fregate Islands.

HISTORY AND CULTURE

Knowledge of the peoples who lived in St Lucia before the arrival of Europeans at the beginning of the sixteenth century is based on recent and on-going archeological and anthropological investigations. What is certain, however, is that this lush and fertile island attracted waves of immigrants from South America who journeyed up the arc of islands from present-day Trinidad to the Greater Antilles, with some putting down roots and settling.

ST LUCIA'S FIRST INHABITANTS

St Lucia's first settlers were Arawaks, Indigenous peoples who travelled up the island chain by canoe from the Orinoco region

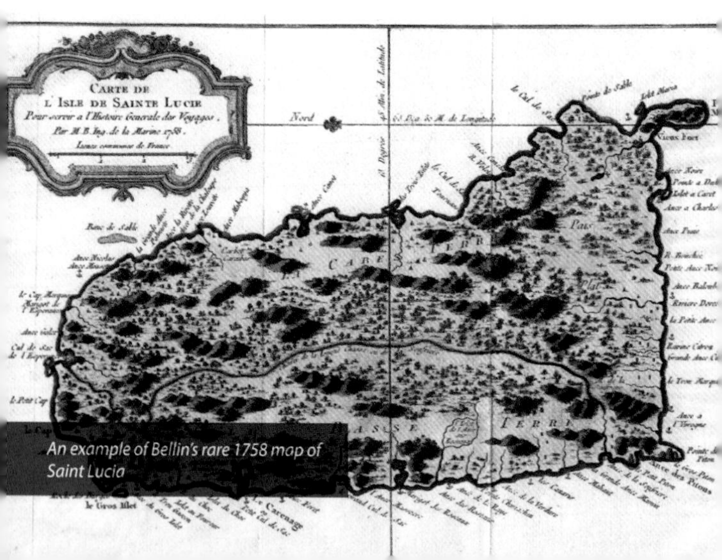

An example of Bellin's rare 1758 map of Saint Lucia

of South America around AD 200. Settlements have been discovered on neighbouring islands which pre-date this arrival, so it's possible that people lived on the island before then, though no evidence has yet been found. The earliest archeological remains have been uncovered at Grand Anse on the east coast and at Anse Noir in the south near Vieux Fort.

A Kalinago family

Some time around 1450, a further flow of migration brought the Kalinago (called Caribs by colonizers), and the Arawaks disappeared from St Lucia – evidence suggests they ceased making pottery after that date. Impressive pre-Colombian petroglyphs – rock boulders carved with art – can be viewed in the grounds of *Stonefield Villa Resort*, along the river at Balenbouche Estate, and at Malgretoute beach.

By the time the Spanish invaded in the early sixteenth century, the Kalinago were the sole occupants of the island they called Iouanalao, meaning 'where the iguana is found'. The name morphed into Hiwanarau, and later Hewanorra, now the name of the international airport in the south.

EUROPEAN COLONIZATION

A degree of mystery surrounds the arrival of the Spanish. Although legend has it that Christopher Columbus discovered the island on St Lucy's Day (13 December) in 1502, his ship's log showed he wasn't even in the area at that time. Despite not knowing who

Rodney attacking the French fleet in 1782

discovered the island, nor when, St Lucy's Day has been adopted as the national holiday. Someone must have spotted it, though, as in 1520, a Vatican globe marked it as Santa Lucía, implying that it was claimed by Spain. It is believed that in the 1550s, the pirate François Le Clerc, or Jambe de Bois, tried to settle on the island and there may later have been an attempt by a Dutch expedition. In 1605, an English ship, *Olive Branch*, landed at Vieux Fort after being blown off course en route to Guiana (Guyana). Of the 67 survivors only 19 were left a month later, when they escaped in a dugout canoe. Naturally, the Kalinago did not take kindly to invasion.

In 1627, St Lucia appeared in a document as one of the territories granted to the Earl of Carlisle. There were no immediate attempts to settle the land and in 1635, the French claimed it had been granted to M. d'Esnambuc in 1626. This was the beginning of a territorial dispute between England and France which was to last until 1814, during which time the island changed hands 14 times.

In 1638 the English made a serious attempt to settle St Lucia, with an expedition of 300 men from Bermuda and St Kitts. They lived alongside the Kalinago for eighteen months until a 1640 dispute led to many deaths on both sides and the English fled. Three years later, the French appointed a governor who was married to a Native American, which allowed him to establish the first permanent settlement. Around this time, the King of France ceded the island to the French West India Company, who sold it to MM Houel and Du Parquet in 1650.

Still the English persisted in staking a claim on St Lucia, while the Kalinago continued to defend their island, killing several governors in the process. Gradually, however, the new, mostly French, settlers introduced a plantation economy using slave labour, growing first cocoa and coffee and then sugar. While the Kalinago were

St Lucians carrying coal onboard a U.S. warship at Castries, 1903

wiped out in St Lucia, they survived on other islands, most notably in Dominica, where a strong community has continuously lived.

EUROPEAN WARFARE

St Lucia was one of many islands fought over by European powers in the seventeenth and eighteenth centuries, being caught up in strategic manoeuvres by governments from far away. While the Spanish were interested in the Greater Antilles, particularly Cuba, for its position on the shipping route between Spain, South and Central America, the English, French and Dutch battled mostly over the Lesser Antilles. One of the most famous battles was in 1782, when Admiral George Rodney led the English fleet from Pigeon Island to attack the French navy off the islands of Les Saintes, intercepting it on its way to attack Jamaica.

The French Revolution, which began in 1789, also had implications for the French colonies, particularly when the new French Republic granted freedom to enslaved Africans in its overseas territories in 1794. Victor Hugues supported insurrections in neighbouring islands from his base in St Lucia. The guillotine was erected in Castries and the island became known as St Lucie La Fidèle by the French. In 1796, General Sir Ralph Abercrombie led English troops in another invasion, fighting a long campaign against a joint force of White and Black Republicans. The newly emancipated islanders, fearing they would be returned to bondage, banded together, joined by a number of French army deserters, to create l'Armée Française dans

British model of government

St Lucia is governed by a multi-party parliamentary democracy based on the British model and led by an elected prime minister. A House of Assembly made up of 17 members is elected for a five-year term and the island's Governor General appoints the 11-member Senate.

les Bois. The rebels – called Brigands by their enemies – led a campaign of resistance across the island. In 1795 they took control of the fortifications on Pigeon Island, but victory turned out to be short-lived. In 1796 British forces defeated and captured them at Morne Fortune.

Banana farmer

The Treaty of Amiens in 1802, which ended the Seven Years' War, returned St Lucia to the French, before it was finally ceded to the British in the Treaty of Paris in 1814. Despite the ideals of the French Revolution, slavery remained in force on St Lucia until the British passed the Emancipation Act in 1834, which came into force in 1838.

BRITISH RULE

From 1838, St Lucia came under the jurisdiction of the Windward Islands Government, with a Governor based first in Barbados and then in Grenada. While important as a plantation economy, from 1885, St Lucia experienced a period of prosperity when it became an important coaling station. Welsh coal was sold to passing steam ships and by the end of the century, Castries was the fourteenth most-important port in the world when rated by tonnage handled. The rise of oil, however, saw the decline of steam ships and a fall in demand for coal, with a resulting adverse impact on the colony's economy.

The 1930s were a period of poverty and labour unrest. In 1935 coal workers went on strike and there was violence which had to be put down by the navy. Two years later sugar workers also came out on strike demanding higher wages. This was the beginning of an organized labour movement, culminating in the formation of the first trade union in 1939: the St Lucia Workers Co-Operative Union. This later grew into the St Lucia Labour Party (SLP), led by George FL Charles (1916–2004), who had championed striking workers and became the secretary of the Union, a reformer and one of the most important politicians of the twentieth century.

In 1951, universal adult suffrage was introduced for the first time and elections that year were won by the SLP. Charles became the first Chief Minister and retained power until 1964. He introduced legislation improving workers' rights and oversaw the shift from sugar production, which had been hit by falling prices, to bananas, which could be produced on smallholdings, benefiting large numbers of small-scale farmers. In 1958, St Lucia joined the West Indies Federation until it collapsed in 1961 when Jamaica pulled out.

The 1964 elections were won by the United Workers Party (UWP), led by John Compton (1925–2007), another prominent politician of the late twentieth century. He held power from 1964 to 1979, then again won elections in 1982, 1987 and 1992, before retiring in 1996. However, Compton came out of retirement to lead the UWP to victory in the 2006 elections, beating the SLP which had lost popularity during difficult economic times and becoming Prime Minister aged 82 until his death a year later. During his first period of

Workers' champion

George Frederick Lawrence Charles came to prominence in 1945 when he championed the cause of striking construction workers who were employed to build an extension to the airport. Knighted in 1998, the airport in Castries was renamed in his honour and a sculpture of the trade unionist was erected there in 2002.

Cruise ships docked in Castries

office, St Lucia gained full internal self-government, becoming a State in voluntary association with Britain. Full independence was gained in 1979. St Lucia remains a member of the Commonwealth with Queen Elizabeth II as head of state, represented by the Governor General.

CHALLENGES IN THE TWENTY-FIRST CENTURY

Although St Lucia produces the largest banana crop in the Windward Islands and has diversified into other agricultural products, such as renovating historic cacao plantations, planting coconuts, growing flowers and promoting fisheries, farming alone is insufficient to sustain the island's economy. As a result, the island has become increasingly dependent on tourism, which has been promoted by the government to provide jobs as well as bring in money. Investment in hotels has been significant, from budget guesthouses to height-of-luxury villas and resorts with correspondingly sky-high prices.

Unsurprisingly, given St Lucia's reliance on the tourism industry, the economic effects of Covid-19 have hit the island hard. Pre-pandemic, St Lucia's enchanting landscape of the Pitons (declared a Unesco World Heritage Site in 2005), spectacular beaches, and wildlife-rich rainforests was on track to attract around a million tourists each year. In fact, 2018 saw the island enjoy a record-breaking year, with 1.2 million visitors recorded – 760,306 cruise travellers and 394,780 stayovers.

After reporting its first case of Covid-19 on 13 March 2020, the St Lucian government declared a state of emergency and closed airports to incoming passenger flights just 10 days later. Though the island opened its borders to travellers from all countries in April 2022, it will take some time for the island to recover fully. That said, the signs are promising, with almost 200,000 stayover visitors recorded in 2021.

GOING BANANAS FOR FAIRTRADE

Banana growers in the Windward Islands benefit from the Fairtrade scheme. It enables small farm owners to pay decent wages to their workers and protect the environment without resorting to heavy use of agrochemicals. They produce less than half the quantity of bananas per hectare produced in the intensive, corporate-owned plantations of Latin America, but in the fragile island ecosystems such levels of output would be unsustainable. At a time when international competition is fierce, with the end of EU quotas because of World Trade Organization (WTO) rulings, the Fairtrade scheme is vital to the survival of St Lucian banana farmers. In 2007, Sainsbury's supermarket in the UK announced that all the bananas it sells would be fairly traded and that 100 million, or 75 percent of the total crop, would come from St Lucia.

IMPORTANT DATES

AD 200 Native Americans arrive in canoes from northern South America.

1450 The Kalinago migrate from South America and settle.

1502 Columbus may have sighted St Lucia.

1550s The pirate, François Le Clerc, tried to settle St Lucia.

1605 The English land in the south after a ship is blown off course.

1627 Land granted to the Earl of Carlisle includes St Lucia.

1635 The French establish a colony, claiming the island was granted to M. d'Esnambuc in 1626.

1638 300 Englishmen from Bermuda and St Kitts settle on St Lucia but flee after 18 months because of battles with the Kalinago.

1659 The English and French commence hostilities. The island changes hands fourteen times in 150 years.

1782 Admiral Rodney destroys the French fleet at the Battle of Les Saintes.

1814 St Lucia is ceded to Britain in the Treaty of Paris.

1838 Following the Act of Emancipation in 1834, slavery is abolished in British territories.

1885 Castries becomes a major coaling station.

1920s The rise of oil and decline of coal lead to economic problems.

1930s Poor working conditions and strikes for higher wages lead to the first trade union.

1951 Universal adult suffrage is established in the British colonies.

1967 St Lucia gains internal self-government as a State in voluntary association with Great Britain.

1979 St Lucia gains full independence.

2005 The Pitons are declared a Unesco World Heritage site.

2014 Negotiations begin with the World Bank and New Zealand to develop geothermal energy at Soufrière.

2020 St Lucia reports its first case of Covid-19 on 13 March and declares a state of emergency.

2022 The island opens its borders to travellers from all countries on 2 April; Prince Edward, Earl of Wessex, and the Countess of Essex, visit St Lucia as part of the Platinum Jubilee tour of the Caribbean.

St Lucia is home to many luxury resorts, as here at Piton Bay

OUT AND ABOUT

The majority of places to stay in St Lucia are concentrated in two areas: in the northwest at Rodney Bay and in the southwest around Soufrière. The former, packed with resorts, best suits travellers seeking easy-access beach activities and nightlife. Surrounded by rainforest, the latter offers a mix of village life, spectacular views of the Pitons, and breathtaking underwater experiences. There are lots of excursions on offer from the north to attractions in the south overland or by sea, but fewer going the other way. While it's feasible to drive around most of St Lucia in a day, hiring a driver is more relaxing than navigating mountain roads yourself, with the benefit of learning more about the island from a knowledgeable guide. Alternatively, use local buses.

CASTRIES AND ENVIRONS

St Lucia's capital, **Castries** ❶, which lies on the western side of the island, has a population of 67,000. It has been razed by fire and rebuilt four times over the years, leaving few old buildings with historic or architectural value. Much of the town is made up of nondescript modern buildings, but Castries still has character and vibrancy, especially on Saturday when the market is awash with locals doing their weekly shopping and curious tourists enjoying the atmosphere and searching for souvenirs. When cruise ships are in port, the capital bulges at the seams.

The Port of Castries is a busy working harbour where container ships can be seen unloading their contents on to the dock at the North Wharf, adjacent to the Place Carenage duty-free shopping mall. When cruise ships are in the harbour they dominate all other vessels and even the surrounding buildings. Fishing boats painted the colours of the rainbow can be seen dodging the big ships as they weave in and out of the harbour in Trou Garnier, while yachts sail in and out of Petit Carenage.

A tour of Castries is best negotiated on foot, as the central area is compact, but a taxi is recommended when you explore the sights such as Morne Fortune on the southern outskirts. Buses are also readily available.

THE TOWN CENTRE

Derek Walcott Square Ⓐ sits at the heart of the capital, bordered by Brazil, Laborie, Micoud and Bourbon streets. This well-kept, small green space, scattered with a few mature trees, was called Place d'Armes in the eighteenth century, when it was the

Port of Castries

site of public executions around the time of the French Revolution. By the late twentieth century, the square had undergone two name changes: it was called Columbus Square until 1993, when it was renamed in honour of Castries-born poet and playwright Derek Walcott (see box, page 30), who won the Nobel Prize for Literature in 1992.

A local staple

Cassava is a root vegetable grown throughout St Lucia. The plant is peeled and grated and the juice extracted, before it is dried to produce farine (a fine flour), which is used to make bread or porridge.

A tall samaan tree with branches laden with epiphytes is believed to be more than 400 years old and offers some shady relief from the tropical sun. A paved pathway runs through the middle, linking a memorial obelisk and plaque to the bandstand at the opposite end. The memorial at the west side of the square honours the memory of St Lucians who fought and died in both World Wars.

Jazz on the Square is a popular event that attracts visitors and locals who gather here for a daily dose of free music during the St Lucia Jazz Festival, held in May. Office workers often use the bandstand and benches here during their lunch hour. At the centre of the square is a fountain and, further back towards the bandstand, are busts of the island's two Nobel Prize winners: writer Derek Walcott (see below) and economist Sir Arthur Lewis.

On the corner of Laborie and Micoud streets is the Roman Catholic cathedral, **The Minor Basilica of the Immaculate Conception** ❸ (open daily, unless Mass is in progress). This has been the site of several churches dating back to the eighteenth century, but the current building was not completed until 1931. Inside there are enough beautiful dark wood pews to seat around 2000 worshippers, intricately carved columns and arches, and a stone altar flanked by displays of votive candles. Yellow light floods the building through decorative windows in the ceiling, which is adorned with a depiction of Catholic saints. Renowned St Lucian artist Dunstan St Omer painted the murals on the cathedral walls

HONOURABLE ST LUCIAN

Born in Castries in 1930, Derek Walcott OBE OCC trained as a painter and writer and studied at the University of the West Indies in Jamaica. In 1953 he moved to Trinidad where he founded the Trinidad Theatre Workshop in 1959. In 1981 he set up the Boston Playwrights Theatre at Boston University, where he worked as Professor of Literature. From 2010 he was Professor of Poetry at the University of Essex in the UK, and published many collections of poems, an autobiography in verse, *Another Life*, critical works and over 20 plays. Standouts include the epic narrative poem, *Omeros* (1990), which contributed to him winning the Nobel Prize for Literature in 1992. In 2011 he won the TS Eliot Prize for his book of poetry, *White Egrets* (2010). In February 2016, Walcott became one of the first knights of the Order of Saint Lucia. His twin, Roderick, was also a playwright, poet and artist, and their childhood home on Grass Street has been declared a heritage site. Walcott died in St Lucia on 17 March 2017.

Castries Central Market

in 1985 in preparation for a visit by Pope John Paul II the following year. The beautiful artwork reveals the Stations of the Cross, with characters inspired by local people. In 2005, St Omer and his son, Giovanni, created twelve magnificent stained-glass windows that were installed on either side of the cathedral.

As you leave the cathedral on Laborie Street, to your left is Brazil Street, lined with a cluster of buildings dating back to the late nineteenth century. The wooden structures retain some lovely gingerbread fretwork detail on their balconies; these, and the buildings behind, were the only ones of their kind to survive Castries' last great fire in 1948.

One of the only other places that escaped the flames in 1948 was the old **Central Market Ⓒ**, situated north of Jeremie Street towards John Compton Highway. Built of iron in 1894, the original market shelter is where you will find the town clock and a modern annexe. Vendors from rural areas sell local produce, such as fresh fruit, plump vegetables, cassava, cocoa sticks, fiery pepper sauces, aromatic spices and basketwork.

Across the road on Peynier Street is the **Vendors' Arcade** **D**, which backs on to the waterfront; you can find an array of souvenirs and gifts here, including inexpensive, colourful T-shirts, beach wraps and some very good basketwork, in both traditional and modern styles.

Head west from the Arcade along Jeremie Street to **La Place Carenage** **E** (Mon–Fri 9am–5pm, Sat 9am–2pm, also Sun if a cruise ship is in town), the duty-free shopping mall packed with a selection of shops selling crafts and souvenirs, boutiques and art galleries. The mall also has a small interpretative facility, the **Desmond Skeete Animation Centre**, which has displays of ancient Native American artefacts and an audio tour. Heading west along La Toc Road you come to the ferry terminal, from where the L'Express des Iles ferry operates a regular and fast service to Martinique, Dominica, Guadeloupe and the outer French islands.

VIGIE PENINSULA

Across the harbour and reached by a regular water-taxi service is the large, upscale **Pointe Seraphine** **F** duty-free shopping mall (Mon–Fri 9am–5pm, Sat 9am–2pm, Sun 9am–4.30pm if a cruise ship is in town), busy at the weekend and even more so when a cruise ship is anchored at the dock next door. Take the inexpensive ferry to cross the water or jump in a taxi for the short drive around the harbour. The walk from here to Castries centre isn't that long, but it can seem so, especially in the heat.

On the **Vigie peninsula** **2** is the George F.L. Charles Airport (formerly known as Vigie Airport), a small landing strip for Caribbean inter-island and domestic flights. As you round the corner to join Peninsular Road, with the airport runway on your left, you will see the raised white tombstones and monuments in the small military cemetery created for the men of the West India Regiment. Vigie Beach runs alongside the road on the right. The entire peninsula was once a military stronghold and the barracks and other nineteenth-century military buildings have been restored.

Vigie Lighthouse G stands at the end of Beacon Road on the peninsula, looming above the northern edge of the city harbour. The glowing light from the red lantern at the top of the 11m- (36ft-) high white tower, built in 1914, can be seen around 50km (30 miles) out to sea. The lighthouse overlooks military barracks, eighteenth-century ruins and a scattering of historic buildings managed by the National Trust. From here on a clear day there are spectacular views across the southern and northern coasts of St Lucia, and Martinique.

Colonial-style buildings overlooking Derek Walcott Square

Sir Arthur Lewis

St Lucia is proud to have produced two Nobel Laureates, the first of whom, Sir Arthur Lewis (1915–1991), was awarded his prize for Economics in 1979 for his theories on development economics.

THE MORNE

The historic **Morne** ❸ area is accessible from the southern end of the centre of Castries. On the way up is the studio and shop of **Bagshaws of St Lucia** (Mon–Fri 8.30am–4pm; tours Sat & Sun by appointment; tel: 758-452 6039). The factory uses traditional silk-screen methods to produce colourful prints on fabric, with motifs inspired by island flora and fauna. Tours provide a lively explanation of the printing process and details about Bagshaws. The company also has shopping outlets at La Carenage and Pointe Seraphine in Castries, and another at Hewanorra Airport.

Next door, Bagshaws has restored **La Toc Battery** (you can self-guide most of the site, or book tours to all areas by appointment; tel: 758-452 6039), a fine example of a nineteenth-century battlement with wonderful views and a pretty garden. Built by the British, La Toc has cannons, underground tunnels and munitions storage rooms where valuable artefacts can be seen. There is also a display of some 900 old bottles and other artefacts, found by scuba divers in Castries' harbour.

On top of the hill is the 29-hectare (72-acre) **Morne Fortune Historic Area** Ⓗ, home to the old military buildings of **Fort Charlotte**. The French began building the original fortress in 1768, choosing 260m- (850ft-) high Morne Fortune because of its unmatched vantage point of the harbour. When they took control of St Lucia in 1814, the British continued the work and strengthened the fortifications. It was they who named it Fort Charlotte. The fort remained an important defensive base until early in the twentieth century. The military barracks and other buildings have been restored and converted. Some now house the Sir Arthur Lewis Community College, named after the island's first Nobel Prize winner, who is buried here. Nearby are the ruins of Apostle's Battery, with a large mounted cannon, built in 1890 to support the fortress, as well as the lookout point at Prevost's Redoubt, a French construction dating from 1782.

At the southern boundaries of the fort complex is the **Royal Inniskilling Fusiliers Memorial**, a monument to the soldiers who battled for this position against the Brigands and the French in 1796. The monument also marks one of the best viewpoints on the Morne, affording stunning coastal views to Pigeon Island in the north and as far as the iconic twin Pitons rising high above the west coast.

Morne Fortune Historic Area

While in the area, it is worth visiting the Goodlands workshop of the St Lucian sculptor and woodcarver Vincent Joseph Eudovic and his artistic family. At **Eudovic's Art Studio and Gallery** ❶ (Mon–Fri 8am–4.30pm, Sat & Sun until 3pm; tel: 758-452 2747) woodcarvers produce smooth abstract carvings. The works are made from the ancient roots and stumps of the laurier canelle, laurier mabouey, teak, mahogany and red and white cedar.

Howelton Estate, the home of **Caribelle Batik** ❶ (Mon–Fri 8am–4pm, Sat 8am–noon, Sun if a cruise ship is in port; tel: 758-452 3785; www.howeltonestate.com/howelton-batik), is a fine example of Victorian architecture with a Caribbean twist. The pretty building on Old Victoria Road has been carefully restored and houses a batik studio, café, chocolaterie and gift shop. The batik studio uses Indonesian techniques to create vibrant designs on

Rodney Bay

British and sea-island cotton. The fabric, printed with images of St Lucia's flora and fauna is then made into clothing, wall hangings and souvenirs.

RODNEY BAY AND THE NORTH

The coastal region to the north of Castries is the island's foremost resort area with sheltered bays on the western, Caribbean side, a range of hotels, fishing communities, a marina, shopping malls, vibrant nightlife and historic landmarks. West of the highway, several hotels and restaurants nestle in the curve of **Choc Bay** and along Choc Beach, which is lapped by the calm waters of the Caribbean. Further north, in Bois d'Orange, residences and a hotel are scattered around the hill overlooking **Labrellotte Bay**.

RODNEY BAY

Taking a left turn off the Castries-Gros Islet highway at the Bay Walk Mall on the left-hand side of the road will lead you to **Rodney Bay** ❹, whose main strip is crammed with banks, ATMs, lively bars, restaurants and small hotels. This is the hip spot for nightlife in St Lucia, being close to hotels, with food outlets serving sandwiches, pizza, steak, seafood and French, Indian, Italian and Caribbean cuisine. The hotels also organize entertainment such as crab racing, fire eaters, steel bands or jazz groups, and several restaurants have live music on certain nights. The shopping in **Rodney Bay village** Ⓚ is the best on the island. The Bay Walk Mall has a range of shops, a casino and a supermarket. There is another supermarket in the older JQ Mall on the other side of the road and plenty of opportunities for sailors to provision their yachts.

At the end of the road is **Reduit Beach** Ⓛ, one of the best stretches of sand on the island. The crescent-shaped beach extends as far as Pigeon Island (see page 39) further north, although it is not possible to walk the length of it because of shipping access to Rodney Bay marina and The Landings yacht harbour. There are lots of hotels here but there is public access to the beach, where visitors can rent watersports equipment, sun loungers and umbrellas. In high season, when the hotels are full, and at weekends, it can become crowded, but there is usually enough space for everyone. If you are looking for tranquillity, come on a weekday in the off season. Licensed vendors work this beach, but if you are not interested in what they have to sell, a polite 'no thank you' is all you need.

Rodney Bay Marina Ⓜ and its harbour were created by digging out a mangrove swamp. The popular marina is well equipped and is considered to be among the Caribbean's best. The **Atlantic Rally for Cruisers** (ARC) is a big winter event. Yachts from all over the world take part in this annual transatlantic rally, setting sail in November from Las Palmas in Gran Canaria to Rodney Bay in St Lucia. The 2,700-nautical mile journey takes anything from 12 to 24 days, and festivities around the marina continue as long as it takes for the vessels to reach their destination.

Why Rodney Bay?

Rodney Bay is named after Admiral George Brydges Rodney, who claimed St Lucia for the British in 1762 and later established a naval base at nearby Pigeon Island, from where he set sail to intercept and defeat the French navy on its way to attack Jamaica in 1782.

GROS ISLET

Gros Islet ❺ (pronounced *grows ee-lay*), just north of the marina, is a small fishing village that during the week is an antidote to the pace of the busy harbour. However, most visitors come to **Gros Islet** Ⓝ for the **Friday Night**

Gros Islet's Friday Night Jump-up

Jump-up, a popular street party when tourists and locals converge on the area. Food and snack vendors line the usually quiet streets; bars and restaurants fling open their doors; and sound systems flood the air with the beat of reggae, calypso and soca. This is a good place to enjoy tasty St Lucian dishes, such as locally caught fried fish, chicken or conch, then dance the night away in the crowded street. Things don't hot up until after 10pm and festivities go on into the small hours. Generally, it is pretty safe at the Jump-up, with police, uniformed and plain clothed, on duty, but it's always best to keep your wits about you.

PIGEON ISLAND

Around the bay from Gros Islet is the **Pigeon Island National Landmark** ❻ (daily 9.30am–5pm; interpretative centre closed on Sun; entrance fee). This was once a separate island, accessible only by boat, but was joined to the mainland by a man-made causeway, completed in 1972. While the resorts now located here have claimed part of the sand for guests, there's still a good stretch open to everyone, with a small parking area and snacks available from vendors who trade close to the beach's public access point.

Operated by the St Lucia National Trust, Pigeon Island is of significant archeological and historical importance. The hilly land that spans 18 hectares (45 acres) is thought to have been inhabited by Native Americans, who used the island's caves for shelter and grew staple crops such as sweet potatoes and cassava (manioc). In the 1550s, the pirate Jambe de Bois (Peg leg) also sheltered in the caves.

Later the site played its part during the eighteenth- and nineteenth-century squabbles between European imperialist powers over control of St Lucia. The island's strategic position and usefulness as a lookout made it a popular choice as a military base. Admiral Rodney established a naval outpost here in 1780. He sailed from this point to defeat the French forces two years later at the Battle of the Saints, which took place off the Iles des Saintes between Guadeloupe and Dominica. The Brigands (see page 21) captured the island and took control of the fortifications in 1795, forcing the British to

Pigeon Island National Park

Pigeon Island beach

abandon St Lucia for a while, but it was retaken in 1798. From 1842 it was used as a quarantine centre, but abandoned by 1904.

By the early twentieth century, Pigeon Island was leased to Napoleon Olivierre from St Vincent, who ran a whaling station. Later, in 1937, the island was rented to Josset Agnes Hutchinson, an actress with the D'Oyly Carte Opera company. There was a hiatus during World War II when the US established a communications station and a naval air station here. In 1947 Hutchinson returned to her house in the south of the island (now a ruin), opening a beachfront restaurant, which attracted a colourful yachting crowd. She finally gave up the lease in 1970 and returned home to Britain in 1976.

Passing through the gates of the park you will be faced with a useful map of the area. The path to the right leads to the ruins of the **Officers' Kitchen** and a little further up the hill is the renovated **Officers' Mess**, which houses the small **Interpretative Centre**.

Artefacts and historical displays explain the history and natural environment of Pigeon Island, but it is past its best.

The Officers' Mess is also home to the **St Lucia National Trust** (daily 8am–4pm; tel: 758-452 5005; www.slunatrust.org). The trust was established in 1975 as the result of a campaign to save the Pigeon Island Landmark from being used for a housing development. Its aim is to preserve the natural and cultural heritage of St Lucia, including areas of outstanding natural beauty, and biodiverse and historic sites such as Pigeon Island, Fregate Island and Maria Islands. Contact the National Trust office for tours of their properties.

In early May, the park is a popular venue for the annual St Lucia Jazz Festival (see page 101). The stage is usually set up near the Officers' Mess, using the ocean as a beautiful backdrop; crowds

Fort Rodney ruins

arrive early to find a good spot on the grass from which to enjoy the shows.

You can take a guided tour or simply wander along the paths and trails at leisure. There is an abundance of flora, fauna and many old buildings, some no more than a collection of stones. On the waterfront, just before you reach the overgrown military cemetery, is the *Jambe de Bois* restaurant, a scenic spot to enjoy a drink, ice cream, or full-on St Lucian lunch. There is a jetty and ferry dock nearby and the lovely beach leads back almost level with the park border and entrance.

On a hill, at the southwestern tip of the park, are the ruins of **Fort Rodney**, which had an excellent vantage point. Today, the fort ruins still afford a good view south towards Castries, but the best lookout point is at 110m (361ft) **Signal Peak**. It's a bit of a climb to reach the peak, especially in the hot sun, but it's worth it for the view over neighbouring Gros Islet and far north to Martinique. There is another lookout at the **Two-Gun Battery**, close to the **Soldiers' Barracks**.

THE FAR NORTH

Located to the north of Gros Islet, **Cap Estate** ❼ lies in hilly land that was once heavily forested. Crops such as tobacco thrived here before the sugar boom of the eigtheenth and nineteenth centuries resulted in the land being cleared to plant sugar cane. The properties that sit on the former 607-hectare (1,500-acre) plantation today are the exclusive homes of the wealthy and luxury rental villas. Residents and guests from the nearby hotels can take advantage of the Sandals St. Lucia Golf and Country Club at Cap Estate (www.sandals.co.uk/golf/st-lucia).

The far north of St Lucia is the driest part of the island and much of the coast is rocky and rough where the waters of the Caribbean

Sea meet the Atlantic Ocean in the St Lucia Channel. There are, however, a couple of pleasant beaches on the northwestern coast, which have inevitably attracted hotel development. The picturesque Bécune Point and the golden sand beach of **Anse Bécune** form the northern edge of Cap Estate. The beach is dominated by a large, all-inclusive hotel, *Smugglers Cove*, but there is public access to the beach and sea.

A little further north, there is excellent snorkelling to be had at **Smuggler's Cove**. With a sheltered beach and rugged cliff landscape, it is often a little quieter than Anse Bécune. *Cap Maison Hotel* maintains a beautiful beach bar and restaurant here (*The Naked*

ART DETOUR

In a mansion house on Cap Estate is **Llewellyn Xavier's Studio** (tel: 758-450 9155; www.llewellynxavier.com), where the work of the St Lucian multimedia artist can be viewed only by appointment. His art is exhibited in the permanent collections of museums and galleries all over the world, including the Smithsonian Institution in Washington, the Metropolitan Museum of Art and the Museum of Art in New York and the National Gallery in Jamaica. Xavier's work can also be seen at the Caribbean Art Gallery (tel: 758-452 8071), at Rodney Bay Marina.

The artist's use of oils, watercolours and mixed media reflects the vibrant colours and rich textures of the Caribbean. The artwork *Environmental Fragile*, which was created from cardboard and other recycled material, was commemorated in a postage stamp issue in 2006.

Xavier's first major work in the 1970s was a series of 25 prints dedicated to George Jackson, a young man whose incarceration in America became an international cause célèbre.

Fishermen) with watersports available for guests.

Beyond this is **Cariblue Bay**, a pretty, golden sand beach, which is home to *LeSport*, another all-inclusive hotel resort.

Cas-en-Bas beach bar

At the far north tip of St Lucia is **Pointe du Cap**. At a little under 150m (470ft) high, in a hilly region beyond the Saline Point residential development, Pointe du Cap provides panoramic views across the north coast to Martinique, west to the Caribbean Sea and east to the Atlantic Ocean. The sea below the sheer cliffs is rough and the land is dry scrub spiked with cacti. To the east is **Pointe Hardy** where paths for walkers crisscross the undulating landscape. The bucolic area around Pointe Hardy and north of Cas-en-Bas is part of the large Sandals Golf and Country Club development.

There are no beaches that can offer safe swimming on this rough, wild and windy Atlantic part of the coast.

South of Pointe Hardy on the northeast Atlantic side of the island is **Cas-en-Bas** ❽, known for its collection of quiet beaches. There are no lifeguards; not all the beaches are well maintained; and the roads leading to this coast are rough and hard to negotiate, but they are ideal if you want a quiet escape away from it all.

To get to Cas-en-Bas, take the road across the golf course, which winds its way to the luxury villa resort, *Cotton Bay*. The road ends here, blocked by private land for development, and you have to continue on foot down the track to the sea. Alternatively, take the Cas-en-Bas Road from Gros Islet. The beaches hook around a sheltered, rocky bay and, though the Atlantic waters can be rough, the swimming and snorkelling are usually good. There is a laidback beach bar, with sun loungers outside and kitesurfing available.

EAST OF CASTRIES

East of Castries is the north's picturesque rural interior that stretches across to the rugged Atlantic coast. The land is largely given over to agriculture and small village communities. If you are starting from Rodney Bay, turn off the Castries–Gros Islet Highway north of Choc Bay and the Bois d'Orange district. The Allan Bousquet Highway leads to the village of Monchy, Babonneau, Fond Assau and Desbarra.

Zip-lining through the forest canopy

South of Monchy, through winding roads, is **Babonneau** in the heart of farmland and plantations. The area around Babonneau and Fond Assau is thought to be the place to which the last group of African-born enslaved people were transported, which probably accounts for the strong African tradition that has been retained.

Fond Latisab Creole Park ❾ (Sun–Fri, tours by appointment; tel: 758-450 5461) is a few miles south

Crayfish

A traditional crayfish pot is made of strips of bamboo lashed together, forming a tube that is laid on the river bed. One end is sealed while the other has a flap to allow access to the creatures caught in the pot. Bait can include fresh coconut.

east of Babonneau via narrow country lanes in the small farming community of Fond Assau. The 4-hectare (11-acre) working farm cultivates nutmeg, cocoa and cinnamon, and produces its own honey. Fond Latisab maintains many aspects of traditional St Lucian culture, some of which stem back to when Native Americans inhabited the land, and practises farm techniques that have been passed on from father to son. For example, local guides are summoned by drumbeat. Even though there is a phone on the farm, much communication is done using the ancient art of drumming. Visitors can watch log sawing done to the beating of drums accompanied by a *chak chak* band (named after the sound made by a local instrument). Log sawing by traditional method requires two men with skill rather than brute force to work the 3kg (6lb) tool. While sawing, the men sing Kwéyòl folk songs, accompanied by the band and the drum beats, which help to maintain rhythm. You can also see local people crayfishing, using traditional bamboo pots, and making cassava bread and farine – a flour produced from cassava grown on the estate. Cassava bread is on sale when there is a tour, and home-grown nutmeg and cinnamon can also be purchased.

Down the road from Fond Latisab, in Chassin, at the foot of La Sorcière hill, is the popular **Rain Forest Adventures** ⓾ (Dec–May Tues–Sun; entrance fee; tel: 758-458 5151; www.rainforestadventure.com). During a two-hour tour, visitors are transported high above the forest in an aerial tram, which provides a bird's-eye view of the landscape. Each gondola carries eight seated people and

Grande Anse

a guide to point out the different plants and trees as you glide through the forest canopy. After the ride you can buckle up to zip-line through the forest, an adrenaline rush which is hugely enjoyable and great fun, with only basic levels of fitness and health required. You can also take a guided nature walk. The Jacquot Trail up **Mount La Sorcière** starts from here, and guides are available for birdwatching hikes up the mountain at sunrise to try to spot the elusive St Lucia parrot, which few visitors see in the wild.

Northwest of Babonneau, the winding Allan Bousquet Highway follows the Choc River, eventually leading to the **Union Nature Trail** ⓫ (daily 9am–4pm; no guided tours at the weekend; entrance fee) on an outpost of the Forestry and Lands Department. The trail loop begins on a path near the ranger station and can be covered in about an hour. It is a short walk (1.6km/1 mile) through dry forest with a few small hills, and can be enjoyed by any relatively fit visitor.

The collection of wildlife on the property is small, but includes native species such as agouti, iguana and the St Lucia parrot. There is also a herb garden growing plants with medicinal properties, which are used as traditional cures.

GRAND ANSE

East of **Desbarra** stretches the beautiful beach at **Grande Anse** ⓬, best known as a seasonal nesting site for the endangered leatherback turtle as well as hawksbill and green turtles. The village of Desbarra is perched on top of a mountain. The paved road stops here, and a 4WD is essential unless you want a very long walk downhill. The beach can be seen in the distance just after the track passes the football field.

The secluded 2km (1.2-mile) strip of sand has reportedly been the target of illegal sand-miners. There have also been attempts to take valuable nesting turtles and their eggs. From March to August the beach is monitored by the **Grand Anse Sea Turtle And Nature Defenders** (formerly the Desbarra Grande Anse Turtle Watch Programme), a community group that works in conjunction with the Ministry of Agriculture, Forestry and Fisheries. There are organized guided

Marigot Bay

Marigot Beach Club

patrols of the beach to monitor the turtles and their nests during the nesting season. These incredible events begin in the early evening and continue until the following morning.

The beach lies at the edge of the Grande Anse Estate, formerly a vast plantation spanning 810 hectares (2,000 acres). Today, much of the estate lands is uncultivated, with cacti and dry forest peppering the hills and cliffs, providing a habitat for rare birds that include the St Lucia wren, the St Lucia oriole and the white-breasted thrasher. Snakes, such as the poisonous fer-de-lance and boa constrictor, and the protected iguana also form part of the estate's endemic wildlife.

MARIGOT BAY AND ROSEAU VALLEY

South of Castries, the verdant St Lucian countryside opens up with wide expanses of farmland bordered by dense forest and threaded by rivers. The Millennium Highway leads south out of Castries and towards the West Coast Road.

Within minutes, the beginning of the semi-industrial area of the **Cul de Sac Valley** appears. At the side of the highway is a green space known as the Millennium Park, used as an open-air venue for a variety of festivities including New Year celebrations. In **Grande Cul de Sac Bay**, beyond the park, is a natural deep harbour and a large terminal and storage facility for Hess Oil.

ROSEAU VALLEY

At the end of the Millennium Highway the West Coast Road starts to climb past the Lucelec power station, which provides the main electricity supply to the greater part of the island. A little further on is the small village of La Croix on the edge of the rainforest. From this village, plantation land stretches away into the distance – this is the **Roseau Valley**. The sprawling Roseau Plantation once extended over both the Roseau and the Cul de Sac valleys.

MARIGOT BAY

The picturesque harbour of **Marigot Bay** ⓭ is off the West Coast Road. There is a small palm-fringed beach and a sheltered natural harbour, which includes a yacht and sailing base, making the bay a popular choice among local sailors and visitors who spend the winter in the Caribbean. On the south side of the bay is a luxury resort and marina, which can accommodate the

Talk to the animals

Marigot Bay was immortalized on the silver screen when it was used as a location for the 1967 Hollywood film, *Dr Dolittle*, starring Rex Harrison.

mega-yachts of the wealthy. The north side of the bay is accessible only by boat, but that small detail doesn't appear to put people off: Marigot Bay is well known for its lively nightlife. As the evening descends, the traffic across the bay increases with boats sailing to-and-fro. An inexpensive and regular water-taxi service operates 24 hours per day. The water around the *Marigot Beach Club and Dive Resort* is ideal for swimming and the resort also fronts the area's best beach. The hotel's restaurant, *Doolittle's*, is named after the film that was shot here in the 1960s.

The eastern part of the lagoon has a small mangrove swamp, a natural site that has been protected with reserve status. A board-walk runs through the mangrove, linking the dock where the water taxis are to the St Lucian-owned and operated *JJ's Paradise Resort*.

At the heart of the Roseau Valley plantation area is the small village of **Roseau**, which stands near farmland once owned by

SUGAR RUSH

Before bananas, sugar was the agricultural mainstay and it is this crop that transformed the lush river valleys in the eighteenth century. The demand for sugar and its by-products, especially rum, from Europe and further afield prompted St Lucian farmers to import enslaved men and women from West Africa to carry out the back-breaking work on the land until slavery was abolished in the nineteenth century.

Successful for a time, St Lucia was forced to diversify in the mid-twentieth century following the introduction to Europe of cheaper sugar produced from sugar beet and fierce competition from high-volume sugar producers elsewhere in the Caribbean. The Roseau sugar refinery struggled on but eventually it too gave up; it was one of the last sugar factories to close in 1963.

Geest before it was broken up and taken over by individual farmers. Today many of the farms form part of an agricultural collective providing bananas for European supermarkets. This is one of St Lucia's main banana-producing regions and contains the largest banana plantation on the island.

Religious art

The small hill community of **Jacmel**, which lies east of the Roseau Valley, has a church with a striking painting of a black Madonna and child and other St Lucian figures by the artist Dunstan St Omer. It is best visited with a local guide, as even in daylight the winding, narrow roads are difficult to negotiate.

RUM DISTILLERY

Cane-sugar production fuelled the rum industry on the island, but by the 1970s sugar cane was no longer being grown here. The Barnard family estate, which operated a distillery in Dennery, entered into a joint venture with Geest and moved to the Roseau Valley. Molasses, the raw material for rum production, is now shipped in from Guyana and today the **St Lucia Distillers** ⓮ (Mon–Fri 9am–3pm; entrance fee; reservations essential 24 hrs in advance, call for tour times; tel: 758-456 3148; www.saintluciarums.com) produces a wide selection of rums and liqueurs. Among the dark rums, look for the award-winning Admiral Rodney, an aged rum which should be knocked back neat, or the Chairman's Reserve, also good on the rocks. Bounty is the dark rum you will see most commonly on the island, while Crystal is the white rum used in cocktails.

The distillery is signposted from the West Coast Road. Travelling from north to south, pass the Marigot Bay turn and Marigot school, and continue until you reach a junction. Take a right along a rough, potholed access road (muddy in the rain); at the end is the rum factory, with a visitors' centre, shop and warehouse. This was also the site of a nineteenth-century, steam-powered sugar mill, with a narrow-gauge railway and steam engine used to transport the cane and molasses. The distillery organizes lively guided tours, which reveal how rum was made in the past and how it is produced today. The tour ends with a rum buffet where you can try the 20 or so products they make, from sweet-flavoured spirits (peanut, coconut, cocoa) to the Denros 160° proof firewater.

ANSE LA RAYE

The West Coast Road weaves through the historically important village of Massacré and descends to sleepy **Anse La Raye ⓯**. Its narrow streets are lined with small shops and houses, while small,

Anse La Raye

brightly painted fishing boats bob in the water along the seafront. Fishermen's huts are peppered along the beach, providing shelter and shade for repairing seines (nets). The pace is relaxed and, as people go about their business, visitors can get a sense of the real St Lucia without the tourist gloss.

Friday evening is a different story altogether, for this is when the village wakes up and comes alive with a **Friday fish fry**. In the early evening the road is blocked off as stallholders set up coal pots and barbecues in front of the fishermen's huts and lay out tables so that people can enjoy their meal in the open air while they soak up the atmosphere. By 9pm the place is packed and loud music punctuates the air while locals and visitors alike walk the length of the road to see what's on offer. On sale are fish caught that day, such as red snapper, kingfish and dolphin (dorado or mahi-mahi), and lobster when in season, along with potfish, conch salad, breadfruit salad and floats and bakes (similar to fried dumplings), washed down with a Piton beer or soft drink. The village bars are also busy, as the usual end-of-the-week crowd is joined by visitors looking to celebrate the fish fry with a pint. Basic public facilities are available near the fishermen's huts.

SOUFRIÈRE AND THE SOUTHWEST COAST

Though tiny, even by Caribbean standards, the island spans a wide diversity of landscapes, from open plains to rolling hills and valleys, ragged mountain ranges and lush rainforest. In places, roads cut through the hills, shaded by mature trees and vegetation, while farms and fishing villages dot the panorama below. The journey from Castries to Soufrière takes about an hour and a quarter, even though the distance between the two places is only about 32km (20 miles). You must have your wits about you if you intend to drive because these winding mountain roads can be unforgiving, with

Friday fish fry, Anse La Raye

steep drops down to the valley below and often mudslides after heavy rain. In places there are stunning views of the coast and the Pitons – Gros Piton and Petit Piton – as the road skirts along the steep cliffs.

Where the road widens in a curve in the road, opposite a stand of trees at **Anse La Verdure**, you'll find **Plas Kassav** 16 (daily 8.30am–7/8pm; tel: 758-459 4050). This family bakery uses traditional methods and some innovative equipment to produce farine (from cassava) and a mouth-watering variety of (gluten-free) cassava bread that is popular with local workers, especially at lunchtime. Several cruise ships and organized tours make this a regular stop, providing people with an opportunity to taste one of the island's specialities. Take your pick from a huge variety of flavours, including coconut, peanut butter, cherry and raisin, cinnamon, salt, saltfish and smoked herring. The bread makes a hearty snack or can be used as an accompaniment to a meal.

A few minutes' drive from Anse La Verdure is **Canaries** (pronounced can-ar-ees), a small village where most families make their living from the fruits of the sea. The name originates from an Native American pot (called a *kannawi*) used by the people who settled here. The **Canaries River** flows through the forest and out to sea here, supporting a handful of waterfalls to the south of the village. Most are hard to find without a guide and require a 30-minute hike, at the very least, to reach them.

A few minutes south of Canaries, off the West Coast Road is **Anse La Liberté**. The land, which is managed by the St Lucia National Trust, extends 56 hectares (138 acres) into the forest. It has around 6km (4 miles) of walking trails, a good beach and some basic visitor facilities. You can also reach it by water taxi from Canaries. Anse La Liberté has historical significance. It is believed that enslaved African men and women living and working on the island celebrated their emancipation here in 1834, hence the name – Anse La Liberté (Bay of Freedom). With a diversity of landscapes – beach, dry scrub forests and rainforest – it's a good birdwatching spot for wildlife fans.

As the road snakes through the hills you can enjoy stunning views of the sea and the spectacular western landscape backed by the magnificent Pitons, which dominate the area, lying just beyond the centre of Soufrière. Before that, **Mount Tabac** comes into view, rising high above the hills and forests to its 678m (2,224ft) peak.

HURRICANE TOMAS

The hilly terrain of the west coast of St Lucia means it is particularly susceptible to mudslides caused by torrential rain, which often lead to fatalities and huge farming losses. In 2010, landslides caused by rain associated with Hurricane Tomas killed 14 people.

SOUFRIÈRE

For many years after the country was ceded to the British, **Soufrière** ⓱ remained little more than a small fishing village, but today it is expanding. The population of the village proper and its environs is now believed to be close to 8,000. Soufrière is a joy to explore on foot, with most sights within a few minutes' walk of the water and plenty of places to eat and drink. Most of the area's attractions are either on or underneath the water, or in and around the rainforest. To the east is **Mount Gimie**, which at more than 950m (3,145ft) high stands above both of the better-known peaks of the Pitons.

Soufrière is St Lucia's oldest town and was the capital when France controlled the island. It stands in the shadow of the island's

Colourful Soufrière

most striking and best-known landmark – the twin Pitons peaks rising majestically out of the sea. Louis XIV of France granted around 809 hectares (2,000 acres) of land to the Devaux family, who ran a successful plantation growing sugar, cocoa, tobacco and cotton on the estate. Descendants of the family still own land and property in the area today.

The famous twin Piton mountain peaks

Enter the village via a small bridge over the **Soufrière River**, which flows to the sea just to the west. On the left is a petrol station, to the right is the town hall and after that, business and residential properties line both sides of Bridge Street, the main road. Modern and colonial buildings stand side by side; painted in pastels, many have pretty balconies with gingerbread fretwork. Most notable is the **Old Courthouse**, constructed of stone in 1898, at the southern end of the waterfront.

The waterfront has a small paved area with seats looking out across the harbour, which is often dominated by the sail-assisted cruise ships that frequent the port for a few hours. The deep harbour drops to 60m (200ft) close to shore so large yachts can dock right at the pier.

At the northern end of the pier is another jetty, the **Soufrière Marine Management Area** (SMMA) office, a water-taxi station and tour office where you can book transport around the coast. Visitors can go to places that are difficult to reach by road, and also to some of the island's best dive sites, as well as join boat trips around the Pitons.

The airy **Lady of Assumption Church**, built in the 1950s, stands at the corners of Henry Belmar, Sir Arthur Lewis and Boulevard streets. It has a simple but attractive design with the lovely altar and pulpit made from dark tropical wood. Be sure to look up above

MARINE PROTECTION

The **Soufrière Marine Management Area** (SMMA), extending from Anse Jambon to Anse L'Ivrogne almost at the foot of Gros Piton, protects the unique marine habitat along the west coast of St Lucia, monitors the coral reefs and water quality, and carryies out scientific research in an attempt to prevent damage to reefs, fish stock, beaches and vegetation.

Its four main protected Marine Reserve Areas (MRAs), for which you will require a permit to dive, are: Anse Chastanet, Rachette Pointe, Petit Piton, Gros Piton (restricted access). Permits can be purchased on an annual or daily basis and are available from the SMMA (www.smma.org.lc, tel: 758-459 5500) and authorized dive operators. To protect the reefs:

- Do not damage or touch the coral while you are snorkelling or diving.
- Do not remove any plants, animals, fish or even shells from the sea.
- Do not feed the fish.
- Tie up only to mooring buoys or anchor at official sandy areas.
- Do not buy souvenirs made from coral; it is illegal to remove it from St Lucia.
- Do not buy souvenirs or other items made from turtle shells.
- Do not litter; dispose of waste in the appropriate bins.

the main doors to see the magnificent pipe organ.

Just in front of the church steps is the **town square** where a guillotine was erected by the Brigands (see page 20) during the French Revolution. On the north side of the square, on Henry Belmar Street, you will find buses for Castries and on the south side, on Sir Arthur Lewis Street, are buses running to Vieux Fort and the south.

Anse Chastanet

Renovated in 2019, the town square is lined by attractive little shops, with shady spots to sit and enjoy a takeaway roti. If you're staying in the area and looking to snorkel or dive, drop into Action Diver Adventures (www.aadivers.net, tel: 758-459-5599), located in Soufrière's *Hummingbird Beach Resort*.

ANSE CHASTANET

Anse Chastanet ⓲ is a national marine park and well-known dive area just north of Soufrière. From town, take a water taxi around the bay and ask your boatman to show you the Bat Cave en route. The *Anse Chastanet Resort* and its sister property, *Jade Mountain*, dominate the beaches and 243 hectares (600 acres) of verdant hill-side here. Spacious and luxurious treehouse-style, open-air rooms built into the hillside look out to the Pitons, and a dive operation, **Scuba St Lucia**, rents snorkelling and scuba-diving equipment.

PADI and NAUI scuba courses are available for everyone, from beginners to the more experienced.

Volcanic black sand fronts the hotel, while the **Anse Chastanet reef**, brimming with colourful marine life, offers the opportunity to walk to a dive site within a few metres of the shore, where there are bright displays of coral, sponges, angelfish, parrot fish and seahorses. North of Anse Chastanet are two fine golden sand beaches, **Anse Mamin and Anse Jambon**. Anse Mamin is ideal for a picnic or a day spent relaxing on the beach and in its clear waters. The beach is backed by forest and former plantation land from where **Bike St Lucia** (tel: 758-459 2453; www.bikestlucia.com) organizes energetic jungle-biking trips along 19km (12 miles) of bike trails through the eighteenth-century plantation. The St Lucia oriole is also often sighted in the forest here.

Diamond Botanical Gardens

DIAMOND BOTANICAL GARDENS

South of Soufrière, old estate houses and hotels cling to the hill-sides, mostly shielded from the road by magnificent trees and bordered by fertile farmland. Head east out of town on Sir Arthur Lewis Street and a few kilometres along a good road you will reach the **Diamond Botanical Gardens**, **Mineral Baths and Waterfall** ⓳ (Mon–Sat 10am–5pm, Sun & public hols 10am–3pm; entrance fee; tel: 758-459 7565; www.diamondstlucia.com). The gardens were originally part of the Soufrière Estate, awarded to the Devaux family in the early eighteenth century by King Louis XIV of France. The original baths were built in 1784 by the Governor of St Lucia, Baron de Laborie, after it was discovered that water from the sul-phur springs was mineral rich and therefore an effective treatment for rheumatism and other ailments. The baths were financed by King Louis XVI for his troops on the island, but they were destroyed during battles with the Brigands around the time of the French Revolution. The bathing pools were restored in 1925, while the garden and other facilities were later expanded to provide a com-munal outdoor pool and individual private baths, for an additional fee. Beyond the baths is the waterfall.

A short trail snakes through the gardens, and useful descriptive signs identify tropical flora such as frangipani, red ginger, hibiscus and a variety of trees laden with coconut, cocoa or other local sta-ples, so a guide is not necessary. A longer and more strenuous hike, which crosses over the **Diamond River**, leads to the old mill and a working waterwheel.

MORNE COUBARIL ESTATE

Morne Coubaril Estate ⓴ (daily 9am–4pm; entrance fee; guided tours; tel:758 726 5248; www.mornecoubarilestate.com) lies less than 1km (0.6 mile) from Soufrière on the Soufrière–Vieux Fort Road, almost opposite the slip road leading to the Sugar Beach (also known as Jalousie Plantation) resort. The 113-hectare (280-acre) working plantation is one of the oldest on the island. It was owned by the Devaux family until 1960 when it was taken over by Donald Monplaisir. The Monplaisir family have attempted to restore and preserve the property and its agricultural traditions. The great house with lovely wraparound verandas is not open to the public because it remains a family home.

Colourful flora and trees, heavy with fruit such as papaya, banana, cocoa, coconut, orange and grapefruit, grow in abundance here. At the Copra House, coconuts are prepared for sale to the St Lucia Coconut Growers Association, a co-op which produces coconut oil, and from here there is a lovely view over the

Morne Coubaril Estate

deep bay nearby. You can also see a fully operational sugar mill where a mule is used to turn the wheel that grinds the sugar cane and produces the juice to make sugar and rum.

La Soufrière Sulphur Springs

Replica wooden quarters reveal how enslaved people were forced to live in basic and cramped conditions. The huts have been reconstructed using traditional methods, with mud and paper on the walls and palm thatch on the roof.

An added extra is the opportunity to experience the adrenaline rush of zip-lining in full view of Petit Piton. Pick from one of eight zip-lines soaring through the estate and a canopy of fruit trees. Morne Coubaril also organizes trekking expeditions on horseback (by appointment) and a choice of rainforest hikes (up to 3 hours) that visit the **Coubaril waterfall**, which is fed by the Sulphur Springs. Though strenuous, the walks are fun with an informative guide and reach a lookout point that provides a panoramic view over Soufrière.

SULPHUR SPRINGS PARK

Off the Soufrière–Vieux Fort Road are **La Soufrière Sulphur Springs** ㉑ (daily 9am–5pm; entrance fee), notable for the pungent odour (hydrogen sulphide), not dissimilar to rotten eggs. The Park contains the most active and hottest geo-thermal area in the

Ripe cocoa pods

Lesser Antilles, and there are plans for the energy to be harnessed to produce electricity.

La Soufrière volcano collapsed more than 40,000 years ago and now produces only the foul-smelling gases and hot water that can reach temperatures of 170°C (338°F), but it is known as a 'drive-in' volcano. The rocky landscape of the geothermal field looks like something from a science-fiction movie, with springs and grey-brown mud bubbling up sporadically.

At the ticket booth, be prepared for vendors who congregate here to offer their wares; official guides also wait to escort visitors, for an additional fee, down a wooden pathway and along some uneven ground. They will give you a rundown of the site and its history. Tour operators offer a package of a visit to the springs, a mud bath and natural spa in a warm waterfall. The concrete bath can get very crowded when a tour party is in, so it is best to go early. Be aware that the mud will stain your clothes.

RABOT ESTATE

At the turn off for the volcano is the entrance for the **Rabot Estate** ㉒ (tel: 758-457 1624; www.thehotelchocolat.com), a recently rehabilitated 56-hectare (140-acre) cocoa plantation owned by the British chocolatiers, Hotel Chocolat. The plantation dates back to 1745 and is the oldest on the island, with some very rare old trees of scientific and chocolate interest. This is a true bean-to-bar experience, as they grow their own cocoa before making it into their own delicious St Lucia chocolate in the UK. Local cocoa farmers also benefit as the estate buys their quality cacao pods at premium prices and guarantees a market for their product while also supplying them with young trees to improve their stock.

There's a luxury hotel on the estate with idyllic cottages and villas in view of the Pitons, together with the *Boucan* restaurant which

NATIVE AMERICAN HERITAGE

The area around Soufrière has been an important settlement for centuries, long before the French or British arrived. The Native American settlers were in awe of the volcano, where the Island Arawaks thought their god, Yokahu, slept and the Kalinago (Caribs) named it Qualibou, or the place of death. Archeological evidence of their presence can still be found on the ground.

There are petroglyphs along paths on both the **Jalousie** and **Stonefield Estates**. The former *Jalousie Plantation* hotel (now *Sugar Beach*) was built amid a wave of controversy when local people, environmentalists and archeologists objected to its location due to its proximity to the Pitons, now a Unesco World Heritage Site, and because it was built on an important Native American burial ground, which is now under the tennis courts.

specializes in all things chocolate, both savoury and sweet (see page 115). You can walk to the site of the 1795 Battle of Rabot, stroll through the plantation tasting the ripe bounty of the mango, guava, soursop and papaya trees, then relax with a soothing cocoa massage using the cacao nibs, oil and butter.

Fond Doux Estate

FOND DOUX ESTATE

South of Rabot Estate is the **Fond Doux Estate** ㉓ (daily 8am–4pm for tours, until 10pm for dinner; entrance fee; tel: 758-459 7545; www.fonddouxresort.com), a working plantation and eco resort. An inexpensive guided tour includes a look at the original plantation house, built in 1864 and renovated in the 1990s, which is currently occupied. Adjacent to the estate house is a colonial-style restaurant, which serves a buffet lunch for tour groups, a bar and a souvenir shop. The grounds, which extend over 55 hectares (135 acres), are planted with coffee, banana, mango, citrus fruits and coconut. Surplus spices, fruit and vegetables are sold in the owners' supermarket in Soufrière. There is still an original worker's house, store house, copra house and coffee-drying area on the property, as well as cottages available to rent.

Cocoa grown here is shipped to the UK and to the United States for use in chocolate produced by the Hershey Food Corporation. The drying racks are still in operation and you will be shown how cocoa sticks are made. These are available to buy in the shop. A leisurely walk through the estate reveals an abundance of bright and fragrant flora such as heliconia, ginger lilies and anthuriums. Trails through the estate lead past ruined military buildings built by French engineers in the eighteenth century, while up on the hill is an old Brigands' hideout.

RAINFOREST MOUNTAIN RESERVES

Most of the mountainous heart of St Lucia has been declared forest reserve, partly to protect wildlife and partly to preserve water supply for the settlements around the coast of the island. In some areas there are trails threading through the verdant forest, maintained by the Forestry Department (tours Mon–Fri 8.30am–3pm; entrance fee; tel: 758 468 5636 or 758 468 5634), and it is even possible to hike from west to east coasts starting from Soufrière.

A simple walk in the rainforest is a rewarding experience, preferably with a Forest Ranger to guide you. Six miles (10km) east of Soufrière lies the village of **Fond St Jacques**, where there are paintings by Dunstan St Omer in the church. From the village, there is a poorly maintained road leading up to a Rangers' station. To reach

Edmund Forest Reserve

Gros Piton summit

it, either use a 4WD vehicle vehicle or walk.

With advance notice, the rangers will escort you through the **Edmund Forest Reserve** to the **Quilesse Forest Reserve** and down to the Rangers' station on the **Des Cartiers Rainforest Trail**, near Mahaut and to Micoud on the east coast. Alternatively, for a shorter excursion, follow the **Enbas Saut Trail** ㉔ from the Rangers' station above Fond St Jacques. This steep but exhilarating route winds down 2,112 steps cut in the hillside to the Troumassée River, providing an opportunity to see elfin woodland, cloud forest and rainforest, depending on your altitude. You will be able to gaze out at the peaks of Piton Canarie, Piton Troumassée and Morne Gimie, while listening to the St Lucian parrot in the trees above you. At the bottom there are a couple of river crossings before you reach a pool with a little waterfall, where you can cool off before the arduous hike back up. Expect to get wet and muddy, especially after rain, which is frequent.

THE PITONS

The Pitons dominate the southwestern landscape around Soufrière. **Petit Piton** (743m/2,438ft) is to the north of Soufrière harbour, while **Gros Piton** (798m/2,618ft) is on the south side of the bay near the L'Ivrogne River. The tall volcanic cones, which are choked in rich vegetation, are undoubtedly the most photographed rocks in St Lucia. A Unesco World Heritage Site, their image appears on everything from postcards to T-shirts and art.

For many people the Pitons offer pleasure simply for their sheer beauty. However, more adventurous spirits want to reach the top. Though Petit Piton is the smaller of the two, it is more difficult to summit because of its steep sides, making climbing ropes essential. A relatively easier option is the trail up Gros Piton, although this isn't a walk in the park either. It is not a pursuit to be tackled alone and you will need to employ the services of a local guide. Contact the Soufrière Regional Development Foundation (tel: 758-459 5500; www.soufrierefoundation.org), or the Gros Piton Guides Association (Fond Gens Libre Interpretative Centre, 40 mins from Soufrière, tel: 758-459 3492; open daily 8am–3pm). Be prepared

The mighty Pitons

for a very early start – most guides recommend setting off and reaching your goal early in the morning before it gets too hot.

Scaling the peak can be thirsty work, so remember to carry plenty of water, and don't forget sunblock and a hat. The time taken to complete the climb can vary; it is generally between three and six hours each way depending on the hiker's level of fitness. From the summit you will be rewarded with sweeping panoramic views over the island, north and south, and on a clear day as far as neighbours Martinique and St Vincent.

The **Tet Paul Trail** is an easy alternative for those not fit enough to scale Gros Piton. This 45-minute walk begins in the **Chateau Belair** community in 2.4 hectares (6 acres) of lush vegetation between Fond Doux and the Gros Piton Trail. Head for Fond Doux and you will see the sign at the entrance to the plantation. You walk through a variety of fruit trees and medicinal plants and can enjoy views of the Pitons, Jalousie beach, the coastline to the south and the neighbouring islands.

Petit Piton

VIEUX FORT AND THE SOUTH

The hour-long drive south from Soufrière to Vieux Fort dips and rises through the hills and valleys, skirting forest and farmland, and passing small fishing hamlets on the southwestern coast.

CHOISEUL

Balenbouche Estate

Choiseul is a good-size town with a developed centre that has a town hall, a church, several schools, a post office and petrol station. The ruins of **Fort Citreon**, a fortress which protected Choiseul Bay, still stands guard over the area, but Choiseul is best known for **La Fargue Craft Centre** ㉕ (tel: 758-454 3226), south of the village. This is where local artisans sell their work, such as clay pots, for which the area is well known, basketwork, woodcarvings, local spices, seasonings and sauces. The centre is on the main road and has plenty of parking space. Ask for directions to the craftsmen's workshops if you want something that is not in stock.

BALENBOUCHE ESTATE

A few miles down the road is the **Balenbouche Estate** ㉖ (daily; entrance fee; guided tours by appointment; tel: 758-455 1244; www.balenbouche.com), which stands proudly on 30 hectares (75 acres) between the Balenbouche and Piaye rivers. It is close to a sprinkling of important historical and archeological sites, and nearby **Morne le Blanc** has a good lookout point. The first European settlement at Balenbouche was established in the mid-eighteenth century.

Today, the great house stands on the site of two previous estate houses. It dates from the mid-nineteenth century and is furnished with an abundance of one-off antiques from that period. There are cottages to rent, a restaurant, nature trail and pretty gardens as well as haunting reminders of its dark past such as the crumbling living quarters of enslaved workers. The old plantation's sugar mill and water wheel was fitted with mechanical works that were shipped from England.

There have been several significant archeological discoveries made on the estate, including pre-Columbian petroglyphs, ceramics and stone tools.

Two dark-sand, rough beaches are **Balenbouche Bay**, just a five-minute walk through the estate, and **Anse Touloulu**, a ten-minute walk.

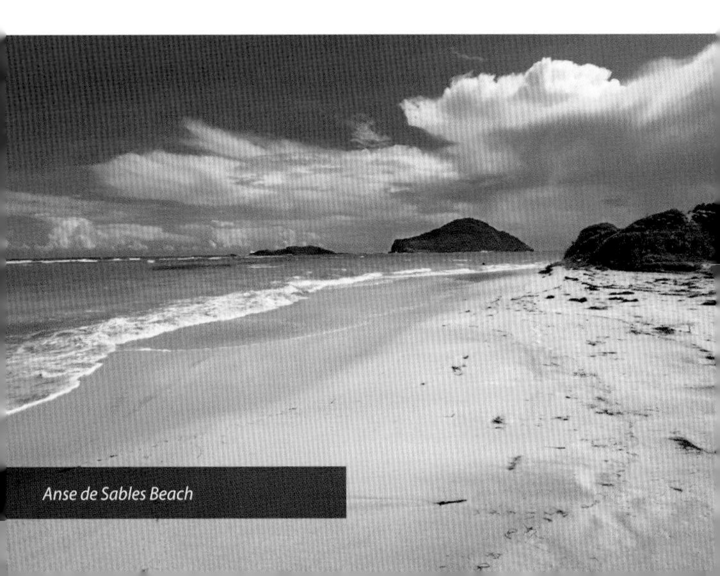

Anse de Sables Beach

LABORIE

The journey continues south-east skirting round and above **Laborie** ㉗, a small fishing community with wooden colonial buildings in its centre and some modern fishing huts on the edge of the water. The village also has the best beach in the area, pretty but quiet, populated by a handful of local fishermen. Laborie has a small selection of accommodation for visitors who prefer to stay away from the crowds, and several good local restaurants.

In the beginning

Hewanorra International Airport is named after a Native American word meaning 'land of the iguana'. There have been significant archeological finds in the south of the island, where the airport is located.

VIEUX FORT

Vieux Fort ㉘, considered to be St Lucia's second city, is one of the oldest settlements. It is draped across the island's most southerly tip, 67km (42 miles) from Castries, with a developing industrial centre and a population of 15,000. **Hewanorra International Airport** is located here, on the plains that open out to the sea. There are a few hotels, mainly B&Bs, not far from the airport, and some developed industry around the large port area, such as oil storage, warehouses and grain stores, and a wharf lined with shipping containers. Here, too, is one of the Eastern Caribbean's commercial free-zone centres and a large fisheries complex, along with a busy, if slightly haphazard, shopping area. Modern villas rub shoulders with fading French colonial-style buildings, reflecting the historical origins of the town's first settlers. The older part of town is full of small grocery stores, typical Caribbean shops, takeaways and bakeries.

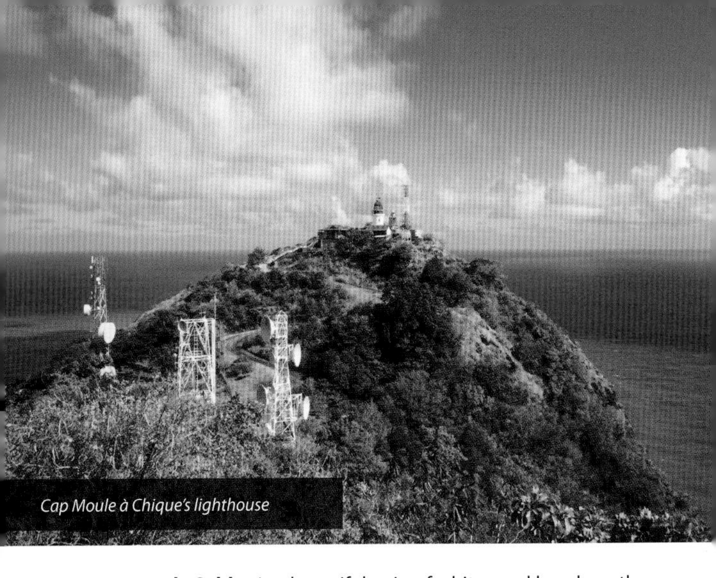

Cap Moule à Chique's lighthouse

Anse de Sables is a beautiful strip of white-sand beach on the east coast of the island. The waters just offshore are popular with windsurfers and kitesurfers who come to take advantage of the trade winds that blast this coast. There is a little bar and restaurant and a surf centre, where boards and equipment can be rented.

CAP MOULE À CHIQUE

Cap Moule à Chique ㉙ is a rocky outcrop with dry forest and a tall lighthouse that towers high above the town, and it is as far south as you can get on the mainland. The drive up to a lookout is twisting and narrow, bordered by vegetation and sheer cliffs. Several residences dot the winding landscape and the peak.

Standing 223m (730ft) above sea level, the 9m- (29ft-) high **lighthouse** tower is believed to be the second highest in the world, because of its location perched on Cap Moule à Chique. Painted white with a red lantern at the top, the tower itself is closed to the public but the lighthouse site is open. From this vantage point the view is spectacular: to the northwest, beyond Vieux Fort, are the rolling hills and valleys of southern St Lucia, including the Pitons in the far distance, and **Morne Gomier**, a 313m- (1,028ft-) high peak closer to town. To the northeast, just off the coast, you will see the rocky Maria Islands Nature Reserve poking out of the sea like seals. Here, too, are sweeping views up around the East Coast, where the waves of the Atlantic Ocean buffet the land and the rocks below. On a clear day you can see the north coast of St Vincent.

MARIA ISLANDS

Maria Islands Nature Reserve ㉚ (closed during the summer breeding season mid-May to end of July) lies 1.5km (1 mile) east of Vieux Fort, across a narrow ocean channel. The two largest islets,

PRESERVING THE WHIPTAIL LIZARD

The St Lucia whiptail lizard (*Cnemidophorus vanzoi*) is not only endemic to St Lucia but is the only whiptail found in the Eastern Caribbean. The males sport the colours of the St Lucian flag: black, white, blue and yellow. Cats, rats and mongooses decimated the population until by the 1960s only a few lizards remained on the Maria Islands offshore.

In the 1990s the Forestry Department and the Durrell Wildlife Conservation Trust began a programme to introduce the whiptail to other predator-free offshore islands. A satellite colony on Praslin Island was hugely successful and this was followed in 2008 by introducing whiptails to Rat Island, on the west coast off Castries, in order to widen the gene pool.

St Lucia racer, Maria Islands Nature Reserve

Maria Major and **Maria Minor**, form the main part of the nature reserve, which covers 12 hectares (30 acres) of dry scrubland and rocky outcrop.

These compact islands on St Lucia's windward side have been sculpted by the rough waves of the Atlantic, and are home to an array of rare bird and plant life. Noddies and terns have protected nesting sites here. Look out for the endemic St Lucia whiptail lizard scuttling under bushes (the male has the colours of the national flag), and the non-poisonous kouwess grass snake slithering through the undergrowth.

Access to the nature reserve is restricted to guided tours run by the St Lucia National Trust Southern Regional Office (tel: 758-454 5014; www.slunatrust.org; see page 42) and to reach it visitors will need to take a small boat across the channel. Take your swimsuit and snorkelling gear as there is a dinky beach and plenty of underwater life.

THE EAST COAST

The East Coast Road from Vieux Fort traces a scenic route along the coastline of the windward side of the island. This is the less commercial part of St Lucia with fewer large resorts and hotels than on the west coast, but a wealth of nature reserves and walking trails through the rainforest, gardens and fishing hamlets.

SAVANNES BAY

North from Vieux Fort is the **Savannes Bay Nature Reserve** ㉛, a protected wetland and the second-largest mangrove swamp in St Lucia (the largest being the nearby **Mankoté Mangrove** ㉜, which lies a little further south). An extensive reef system runs from near the Maria Islands (see page 77) to the north end of the Savannes reserve. The protective reef allows for the cultivation of sea moss, which is grown on ropes beneath the water, suspended by hundreds of plastic bottles. A wealth of birdlife, such as herons, terns and egrets, inhabits the rich mangrove swamp.

Hiking in the rainforest

Until the 1960s the Mankoté Mangrove and forest were part of a US military base that stretched across more than 1,200 hectares (3,000 acres). Due

Savannes Bay

to restricted access to the land, the mangrove swamp suffered little or no damage caused by development elsewhere. However, once the US vacated the land, the swamp was opened up to commercial fishermen and hunters, until it was granted reserve status by the government in 1986.

Nearby **Scorpion Island**, cast adrift in Savannes Bay, also contains a tangle of red and black mangroves.

Around 16km (9 miles) from Vieux Fort is **Micoud**, a small coastal village and an ideal place to visit during two of the island's biggest religious festivals, La Rose in August and La Marguerite in October. They are both celebrated with church services, street parades, delicious food and fun events.

Inland is the starting and ending point for hikers attempting the walking trail that runs across the island through the Quilesse Forest and Edmund Forest reserves to Fond St Jacques, just outside Soufrière (see page 58). Alternatively, the circular **Des Cartiers Rainforest Trail**, at the start of the route, is about 4km (2.5 miles) and takes two hours to complete. There are no steep hills, but the path can be muddy and slippery after rain. Guides at the Rangers' station can escort you. Parrot watching is good here in the early morning, but you must make arrangements with the Forestry Department (tours Mon–Fri 8.30am–3pm; entrance fee; tel: 758 468 5636 or 758 468 5634) beforehand.

West of Micoud and north of the Troumassée River is **Latille Waterfall** ㉝ (entrance fee), which has 6m (20ft) cascades that rush into a pool below; bring your swimsuit.

MAMIKU GARDENS

Mamiku Gardens ㉞ (daily 9am–5pm; entrance fee; tel: 758-455 3729; www.mamikugardens.com) has five hectares (12 acres) of grounds wrapping around an old estate house. It is located off the main road just north of Mon Repos in the Micoud Quarter, not far from Praslin Bay. In the eighteenth century, the Mamiku Estate was home to a French governor of the island; it later became a British military outpost during the tussle for ownership. Visitors to the tropical gardens can explore a series of self-guided walking

Mamiku Gardens

trails lined with orchids, heliconia and hibiscus and shaded by trees, including the gommier, which is still used to make dug-out canoes. A small herb garden includes plants used in bush medicine introduced to the island by enslaved West Africans. Also on the site are ruins and archeological artefacts. There is parking, a snack bar and a gift shop, and the ticket booth has trail maps.

PRASLIN BAY

Praslin Bay ㉟ is a beautiful deep bay carved into two sections by a small promontory which stretches out like a crooked finger towards the tiny **Praslin Island** offshore. The St Lucian whiptail lizard was introduced here from the Maria Islands in 1995 to conserve the species.

Dennery bay

In the southern part of the bay, the village of Praslin maintains the fishing tradition on which it grew, and boat builders construct canoes from gommier trees using ancient techniques believed to have been imported by the first Native American settlers.

The area's extensive red mangroves and mature trees are the habitat of the harmless endemic boa constrictor, a snake that can grow to over 3.5m (12ft). More than 30 species of bird live here and on the islands, such as the St Lucian oriole, the great white heron and the red-billed tropic bird.

Beyond the mangroves and dry forest is a cave network with evidence of a Native American settlement. Petroglyphs and remnants of ceramics and tools have been discovered along these parts.

FREGATE ISLANDS

Just off the coast at the northern perimeter of Praslin Bay is the **Fregate Islands Nature Reserve** ㊱. The two small islands that form the reserve, **Fregate Island Major** and **Fregate Island Minor**, have a combined size of less than 0.5 hectare (1 acre). The islands are named after the frigate bird (*fregata magnificens*), which nests and roosts here, migrating from Cape Verde in Africa, but unfortunately their numbers have dropped dramatically. The islands are covered mostly in xerophytic vegetation, cacti, mangrove forest and grass. The National Trust manages this reserve and Praslin Island, but there are no tours.

DENNERY

The East Coast Road soon reaches **Dennery** ㊲, notable for its fishing industry. This is another village with a lively seafood fiesta (Sat 4pm) held on the beachfront with lots of children's activities as well as food, drink and music.

Inland, along the Dennery River, is the **Rainforest Canopy Adventure** 38 (Errard Road, daily 10am–4pm; reservations essential; tel: 758-458 0908; www.adventuretoursstlucia.com). Instructors strap you into a harness and you whizz down the hill-side on zip-lines suspended high above the forest floor. Also on offer are bike tours along forest trails to the waterfall for bathing, offshore kayaking and a jeep safari, all with knowledgeable guides.

FOND D'OR BAY

About 1.6km (1 mile) from Dennery, where the main road turns west into the Mabouya Valley, is **Fond D'Or Bay**. This crescent-shaped bay is laced by a curve of white sand, backed by sheer cliffs and a rugged landscape. Swimming is not recommended because

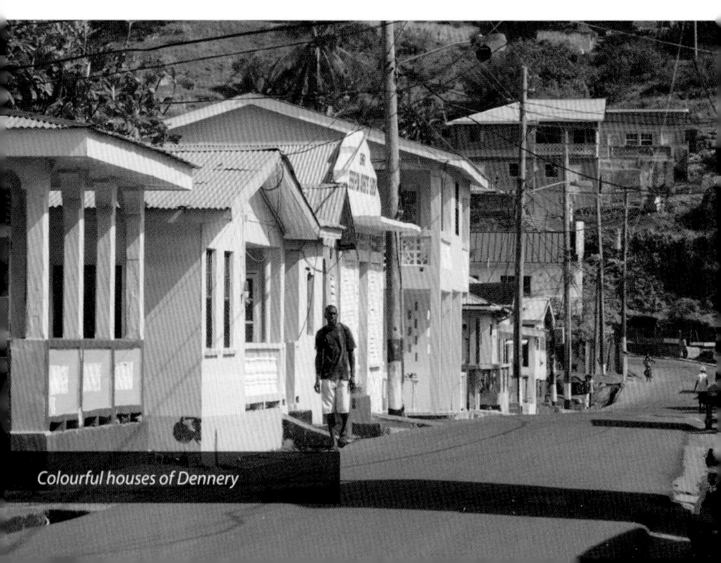

Colourful houses of Dennery

of the rough sea, but the beach is lovely.

Driving from Dennery, the view of the bay from the roadside lookout point is spectacular. Nearby, an old fort and plantation ruins have been developed as **Fond D'Or Nature Reserve and Historical Park** 39 (daily; entrance fee; tel: 758-453 3242), with a wooded canopy of coconut palms, an estuarine forest and mangrove wetlands. Visitors can hike along the forest trails and tour the estate that contains the ruined sugar mill, windmill and the old planter's house, now an interpretation centre. From one of the trails on the edge of the estate, walkers might spot the hill known locally as **Mabouya** or **La Sorcière** (the sorceress), which stands almost 7km (4 miles) away in the Castries Waterworks Forest Reserve.

St Lucian whiptail lizard

TRANSINSULAR ROAD

The road now heads inland and uphill into the forest before climbing over the **Barre de l'Isle**, the ridge which divides the island. At the high point is a stall where Forestry Department guides meet hikers. You can tackle the short **Barre de l'Isle trail** 40 on your own, or hire a guide for the longer **Mount La Combe** hike. As you emerge from the forest the landscape becomes progressively more built up until the smell from the coffee-roasting factory notifies you that you have arrived on the outskirts of Castries again.

Marigot Bay at sunset

THINGS TO DO

SPORTS

WATERSPORTS

The west coast of St Lucia is blessed with the warm, calm Caribbean Sea, making it ideal for a wealth of watersports, with something for all levels of expertise. The east coast, however, is fronted by the Atlantic Ocean, which means potential for high winds and waves – great for surfing adventures, but unsafe for swimming.

Diving and snorkelling

Experienced divers can enjoy rich, colourful marine life in St Lucia, just a few yards from the beach in some cases, while learner-divers can take to the water confidently with an expert instructor. In good news for beginner snorkellers, some of the island's most incredible underwater landscapes can be explored close to shore. Think enchanted kingdoms of colourful coral and sponges populated by the likes of angel fish and seahorses, octopus and turtles. In addition, several shipwrecks around the coast provide fascinating artificial reefs brimming with sealife.

Some of the island's most beautiful dive sites are located in protected marine areas such as the Soufrière Marine Management Area (SMMA). **Anse Chastanet Reef** attracts novices and experienced divers; the marine life is just a short walk in the water from the volcanic sand beach, and there are caves to explore in the relatively shallow parts.

Many of the larger hotels have dive centres on site, while others can offer dive and accommodation packages with independent operators. **Dive Fair Helen** is a long-established, locally owned operation in Marigot Bay (tel: 758-451 7716, www.divefairhelen.com). **Dive Saint Lucia** (tel: 758-451 3843, www.divesaintlucia.com) has a purpose-built training pool and classrooms at Rodney Bay marina. **Scuba St Lucia** is on the beach at *Anse Chastanet Resort*, Soufrière (tel: 758-459 7755, www.scubastlucia.com), with the marine park on its doorstep.

Snorkellers of all ages will find schools of colourful fish and other marine life around Anse Mamin, just north of Anse Chastanet and at Anse Cochon, south of Anse La Raye. North and south of Petit Piton, Malgretoute and Beausejour are also excellent spots for snorkelling.

Kayaking

Exploring the island's coast, rivers and mangrove swamps by water can be a richly rewarding experience. Many kayaking tour guides are able to combine water-based fun with birdwatching, visiting historical sites, snorkelling, and lunching on beautiful beaches. **Dive Fair Helen** (Marigot Bay, tel: 758- 451 7716, www.dfhkayaking.com) offers a variety of tours, most starting from Marigot Bay, where you can explore the mangroves or Roseau River before heading north to Castries, Rat Island or as far as Pigeon Island, or turning south to Anse Cochon.

If you're based in the Soufrière area, **Jungle Reef Adventures** (Anse Chastenet, tel: 758 459 7755, www.junglereefadventure.com) offers a wealth of kakaying experiences, from scooting around the Soufriere Bay coastline and seeing the Fairyland reef site up close, to an exhilarating paddle to the Pitons for more experienced kayakers. It also offers a trip to a fishing village with beach picnic, a romantic sunset kayak jaunt, and birdwatching.

Windsurfing and kitesurfing

The southern coast is a magnet for experienced and adventurous windsurfers and kitesurfers who are attracted by the challenge of the strong winds that can whip up the Atlantic waves off Anse de Sables at Vieux Fort.

The best winds blow from December to June, when the trade winds are most consistent and they blow strongly cross-onshore from the left. That said, you may still catch a good breeze in the summer months.

Reef Kite and Surf (Anse de Sables Beach, Vieux Fort, tel: 758-454 3418, www.slucia.com/windsurf; www.slucia.com/kitesurf) has plenty of equipment for rent and offers windsurfing and kitz-boarding instruction. The centre has good links with several hotels on the island.

Elsewhere, Cas-en-Bas in the northeast is also a popular wind-blasted spot and there are facilities here too offered by **Kitesurfing St Lucia** (Cas-en-Bas, Gros Islet, tel: 758-714 9589, www.kitesurf-ingstlucia.com).

Less experienced wind-surfers may prefer the calmer Caribbean Sea on the west coast. You can rent windsurf boards or kitesurf-ing equipment, and take lessons at the watersports facilities of the larger hotels and resorts.

Diving over stunning coral

Fishing

The warm Caribbean waters are teeming with fish and, depending on the time of year, you could reel in big game fish such as marlin, wahoo, kingfish, sailfish and dorado (mahi-mahi, also known as dolphin); tuna and barracuda can also be caught in these waters. Deep-sea or sport fishing is very popular, and every year there are numerous events and competitions attended by local and visiting fishermen. Visitors can book an entire day or a half-day fishing trip with companies such as **Captain Mike's** (Vigie Marina, Castries, tel: 758-452 7044, www.captmikes.com) or **Hackshaws Boat Charters** (Vigie Marina, tel: 758-453 0553, www.hackshaws.com).

Whale-watching

Around this tiny island, many species of resident and migratory whales can be seen in the balmy Caribbean Sea. The various species can be seen at different times of year, especially during the migratory mating season from October to April. Most common

Jungle-biking: not for the faint-hearted

are sperm whales, pilot whales, humpback whales and false killer whales. Common, spinner, spotted, striped and bottlenose dolphins can also be spotted accompanying the whales, sometimes leaping above the water. The fishing companies above also offer whale-watching tours.

Sailing

An exciting way to explore the coast and see the scenic landscape is by boat. Boat tours can include a spot of diving, snorkelling, swimming or sport fishing, and can be day or sunset party cruises. Full- and half-day sails can be arranged through one of the local boat charter companies based at the marinas at Castries, Rodney Bay, Marigot Bay and Soufrière. One of the oldest and finest, offering catamaran tours, is **Carnival Sailing** (tel: 758-452 5586, www.carnivalsailing.com).

Depending on the time of year, St Lucia hosts numerous sailing events, many of them beginning or ending at Rodney Bay Marina (see www.igymarinas.com/marinas/rodney-bay-marina). There are races round the island, to Martinique and back, or just off Reduit Beach. Meanwhile, the annual Atlantic Rally for Cruisers sees sailors embark on an epic race from the Canary Islands to St Lucia.

LAND SPORTS

Cycling

There are mountain-bike trips on the trails of **Treetop Adventure Park** (tel: 758-458 0908, www.adventuretoursstlucia.com) that run through the scenic countryside and dense beautiful forest, and stopping for a dip in the cooling Dennery waterfall. Not for the faint-hearted are the bike trails that cut through the lush vegetation on the Anse Mamin Plantation. **Bike St Lucia** (tel: 758-457 1400, www.bikestlucia.com) has trails for all levels of experience.

They vary in difficulty from yellow (lower intermediate), red (intermediate) to black (expert). The most challenging ride is Tinker's trail, which has a steep uphill and fast downhill track.

Hiking

Exploring the island interior on foot is one way to experience some of the breathtaking scenery that makes up the volcanic island's landscape. With almost year-round warm sunshine and summer temperatures rising above 31°C (88°F), the high mountain and forest areas, where it is several degrees cooler, provide walkers with welcome relief from the heat.

St Lucia has 77 sq km (30 sq miles) of protected forest land, which is the natural habitat of rare plants, trees, birds and wildlife. As a result, walking tours are permitted only with an official guide. Forest walks and hikes vary in difficulty.

The **Edmund Forest Reserve** has a manned ranger station and a public toilet. A three-hour hike along the reserve's strenuous walking trails leads deep into the forest, where you can enjoy

HOWZAT

The official cricket season runs from January to July when there are inter-island, regional and international matches. There is an impressive national cricket ground in Beausejour, Gros Islet, the venue for some of the Cricket World Cup matches when the tournament was hosted by the West Indies in 2007. The ground was renamed the Daren Sammy Stadium in July 2016 in honour of the Windies captain who led the team to victories in the 2012 and 2016 ICC World T20. The Micoud-born cricketer was the first St Lucian to be selected for the men's senior Windies team. Female St Lucian cricketers are also valuable members of the West Indies team.

Hiking along a waterfall-dotted river

the shade of tall ferns, blue mahoe, bamboo and mahogany laced with bromeliads, lianas and orchids. You can also see fabulous flora and fruit such as the bird of paradise, brightly coloured heliconia and hibiscus, banana and pineapple plants.

Visitors need to be fairly fit to attempt the 4km (2.5 mile) **Enbas Saut Trail**, which takes walkers down 2,112 steps to two cascades that flow into clear pools below, and beyond to the Troumassée River and the sleepy hamlet of Micoud on the East Coast. Nearby, the lush, canopied Quilesse Forest Reserve is the habitat of the rarely seen St Lucia parrot (*Amazona versicolor*), known locally as jacquot. The walking trails through this reserve can also provide glimpses of other indigenous island wildlife.

The moderately taxing **Barre de L'Isle Trail** (1.6km/1 mile) cuts through the forest in an east to west direction and provides unforgettable panoramic views over the Cul-de-Sac and Mabouya valleys and out to the Atlantic Coast. A short drive (30 minutes) southeast of Castries is the 5km (3-mile) **Piton Flore Nature Trail/ Forestière Trail**. It follows an old French road through a mature forest with lush ferns and fig trees.

For more information about the island's forest reserves and other national heritage sites, or to book a trail hike, contact **St Lucia Forestry Department** (tel: 758-468 5636, www.govt.lc).

Birdwatching

With such vast forested areas and a mountainous landscape, St Lucia is an excellent destination to spot rare, indigenous and migratory birds. The island has the Eastern Caribbean's highest number of endemic birds – St Lucia parrot (*Amazona versicolor*), St Lucia pewee (*Contopus latirostris*), St Lucia warbler (*Setophaga delicata*), St Lucia oriole (*Icterus laudabilis*), St Lucia black finch (*Melanospiza richardsoni*), and the critically endangered Semper's warbler (*Leucopeza semperi*).

With patience and luck you may also see the endangered St Lucia wren subspecies (*Troglodytes aedon mesoleucus*), and the White-breasted thrasher (*Ramphocinclus brachyurus sanctaeluciae*). Both are endemic to the Lesser Antilles, and both may well warrant full-species status in time. St Lucia is also home to three

Green-throated carib

hummingbirds – the purple-throated carib, green-throated carib and Antillean crested hummingbird.

Notable birdwatching sites include the Millet Bird Sanctuary, Edmund Forest Reserve, Quilesse Forest Reserve, Grand Anse, Grand Bois Forest, Maria Islands Nature Reserve, Savannes Bay Nature Reserve and the Monkoté Mangrove swamp.

Birdwatching tours are best arranged through the Forestry Department (tel: 758-468 5636). Alternatively, Anse Chastanset Resort offers birdwatching packages and has an on-site bird guide (see www.ansechastanet.com/activities/birdwatching).

ATV tours

A tour on an all-terrain vehicle (ATV) adds a touch of adventure to any trip. Based in Soufrière, **Island ATV** (tel: 758-284 4400, www.island-atv.com) offers trips from the southern mountains through lush valleys, an old plantation and Devil's Bridge to stunning black sand beaches.

Zip-lining

There are several places offering zip-lining in addition to other attractions on site. **Rain Forest Adventures** (Chassin, tel: 758-458 5151; www.rainforestadventure.com) has some good lines through the forest in the northeast, while also offering a canopy tram tour, hiking and birdwatching.

On the west coast, in full view of the glorious Pitons, **Morne Coubaril Estate** (Soufrière, tel: 758-459 7340; www.stluciaziplining.com) has zip-lines wending through the plantation and its fruit trees, as well as tours of the estate, hiking to a waterfall and horse riding excursions.

On the east coast, along the Dennery River, is **Treetop Adventure Park** (Dennery, tel: 758-458 0908; www.adventuretoursstlucia.com), with zip-lines suspended high above the forested hillside, as well as a selection of bike tours, kayaking excursions and a thrilling jeep safari.

Golf

Two of St Lucia's Sandals resorts have golf courses. The Sandals La Toc Golf Club offers a 9-hole, par 33 course, while the Sandals St Lucia Golf and Country Club at Cap Estate has an 18-hole, par 71 championship course designed by Norman Foster (tel: 758-721 8672, www.sandals.co.uk/golf/st-lucia).

SHOPPING

There are two pricey shopping malls in Castries designed to attract cruise-ship visitors: La Place Carenage and Pointe Seraphine,

Shopping at Caribelle Batik

while in Rodney Bay there is Baywalk Mall with a variety of interesting shops and a supermarket opposite the older JQ Mall, which also has a well-stocked supermarket.

For souvenirs and gifts such as cocoa sticks, spices, hot sauces and other local specialities, try the market in Castries, at its busiest on a Saturday morning when farmers come to town. Crafts, T-shirts, hats, sarongs and beach wraps can be found in the Vendors' Arcade across the road (see page 32).

Christmas fireworks

A familiar sound at Christmas time in rural hill areas is the loud crack of bamboo bursting. Traditionally young men hollow out a piece of bamboo, insert a stick and plug the bamboo with a kerosene-soaked rag. When lit the noise of the bamboo bursting can be heard far away.

ART

St Lucia has no national gallery, but exhibitions of the work of local artists are mounted regularly. The **St Lucia National Archives Portrait Gallery** (Clark Avenue, Vigie; tel: 758-452 1654) has changing exhibitions of photographs and portraits of eminent St Lucians from all walks of life, some painted by the most famous local artists, Cedric George and Dunstan St Omer.

Commercial galleries include: **Art and Antiques** (Pointe Seraphine, Castries, tel: 758-459 0891) exhibits the work of Llewellyn Xavier and other local and international artists; **Artsibit Gallery** (corner of Brazil and Mongiraud streets, Castries, tel: 758-452 7865) has paintings, sculpture, prints and pottery from St Lucia and the Caribbean; and **The Inner Gallery** (Reduit Beach Avenue, Rodney Bay Village, tel: 758-452 8728, www.facebook.com/theinnergallery) has a selection of work by local artists from St Lucia and the Caribbean.

View of the Pitons

CRAFTS

African-influenced art and crafts can be found in artists' studios, markets and souvenir shops around the island. Revered sculptor and woodcarver Vincent Joseph Eudovic has worked at his Goodlands studio in the hills of Morne Fortune since 1975 (tel: 758 452 2747, www.eudovicsart.com; see page 34). His beautiful abstract carvings are created from local woods such as laurier mabouey, teak, mahogany and red and white cedar.

London-born Simon Gajadhar, known as Zaka, settled in St Lucia after visiting his father's home island back in 1993. A former shipwright, Zaka uses traditional woodcarving techniques to create incredible, intricate masks and totems. While his vibrant work is displayed and sold island-wide, you can't beat visiting *Zaka's Art Café* to see the man at work, and to enjoy some of the best coffee on the island (Sulphur Springs Road, Malgretoute, tel: 758-457 1504).

Choiseul is well-known for its distinctive clay pottery but also for its fine hand-woven baskets that are sturdy enough to take to market and aesthetically pleasing enough for an excursion to the beach. The craft centre at Choiseul (see page 73) sells the work of local potters, basket-weavers and woodcarvers, who breathe new life into age-old crafting traditions handed down from generation to generation.

The ancient Indonesian art of batik is given a Caribbean twist at Caribelle Batik. Fabric is printed with bright images taken straight from St Lucian wildlife and natural landscapes.

ST LUCIA FOR KIDS

St Lucia is the ideal family holiday destination, with no shortage of ways to entertain children and older teens. The powder-soft

KWÉYÒL FLOWER FESTIVALS

The twin flower festivals of La Rose and La Marguerite, held respectively on 30 August and 17 October, have important historic roots. La Rose and La Marguerite are floral societies which some St Lucians align themselves to, pledging allegiance to either the rose or the marguerite flower. While these are now singing and cultural groups, they have their origins in secret societies set up by enslaved African communities. Both occasions are marked by a colourful fête packed with pageantry, with an appointed King, Queen and their court overseeing their society to the spirited singing of a "shantwel".

Contact the Patrick Anthony Folk Research Centre (tel: 758-452 2279; www.facebook.com/saintluciafolk) for news on upcoming cultural events.

Caribbean beaches come in a range of sand colours, lapped by bathwater-warm shallows to play in. Watersports centres cater for all ages, and children will love learning to windsurf, sail or kayak. Snorkelling and diving is incredibly exciting, especially for that first glimpse of the vibrant underwater landscape. On land, thrill-seekers can get their kicks on a zip-line or mountain bike, or burn off some energy with a wildlife-spotting hike through the rainforest. A favourite activity is learning about geology through the mud and nasty smells at the Sulphur Springs. Whale-watching and turtle-watching trips are also fantastic learning experiences.

The food is great, with plenty of tropical fruits and juices to balance out the pizza, pasta and burgers. Health is rarely an issue, as long as children are kept hydrated and protected from the sun; avoid the peak of day (even if cloudy), especially for boat trips.

Soufrière Sulphur Springs

WHAT'S ON

January Nobel Laureate Week (3rd week). Talks and lectures celebrating the two St Lucian Nobel Laureates, both born on 23 January: Sir Arthur Lewis and Derek Walcott.

22 February Independence Day, celebrated with exhibitions, sporting events, concerts and talks.

May St Lucia Jazz Festival (variable), held at a variety of mostly outdoor venues. Concerts by local and international artists attract large crowds.

29 June St Peter's Day. Fishermen's Feast (Fete Peche) when all the fishing boats are decorated.

June, July Carnival (variable). St Lucia Carnival is a fun-filled celebration culminating with Mas Bands 'jumping-up' in colourful costumes and calypsonians vying for the crown of the Calypso Monarch.

30 August Feast of St Rose de Lima (La Rose, Fêt La Wòz). Dancing and singing by communities in traditional costumes.

October Thanksgiving Day (first Monday). Giving thanks for hurricane survival or the lack of a hurricane.

17 October Feast of La Marguerite. A church service followed by a parade with participants dressed as kings and queens, as well as music, dancing, food and drink.

October Jounen Kwéyòl Entenasyonnal (International Creole Day; last Sun). Activities are held throughout Oct but culminate with celebrations on the last Sun of the month in four or five communities with local food, crafts, music and cultural displays.

December Atlantic Rally for Cruisers. Cruising yachts kick off in Las Palmas, Gran Canaria, in November and race all the way to Rodney Bay, arriving the month before Christmas for a season of riotous parties and fun-filled celebrations.

13 December National Day. St Lucy's Day, the patron saint of light is celebrated with the Festival of Lights and Renewal and a procession illuminated with lanterns.

25 December Christmas Day. A Christmas tradition is the equivalent of carol singers, who sing Creole songs to music from a chak chak band.

FOOD AND DRINK

In almost every aspect of St Lucian culture there is a colourful blend of African, Native American, French and British influences, and nowhere more so than in its Creole cuisine. The tropical climate and fertile soil mean that the island enjoys a near endless bounty of nature, from cassava, sweet potato and dasheen to fragrant nutmeg, cinnamon and ginger. The landscape is punctuated with rich farmland where bananas, pineapple, grapefruit, oranges and mangoes grow in abundance.

There is also superb seafood from the surrounding Caribbean Sea and Atlantic Ocean. The market in Castries is a riot of colour and scents, well worth exploring to investigate the wealth of

Spicy sauces for sale in Castries

Catch of the day

produce grown on the island or gathered from its surrounding waters. It is a feast for the eyes and nose as well as the taste buds; you can buy fruit and snacks for a picnic, sample a local lunch at a market stall or stock up on cocoa and spices to take home as edible souvenirs.

A typical lunch will include meat of some sort, served with plantains, potatoes or other starchy vegetables, macaroni, rice and shredded lettuce, all washed down with fresh fruit juice. This is typically the main meal of the day.

Most of St Lucia's restaurants in the tourist areas also serve a range of international or fusion cuisine. You can savour the very best beef steaks imported from the USA or Argentina, share a huge pizza with friends, grab a burger or go for a curry. The island cannot support livestock farming to any great degree, so beef, lamb and dairy produce is usually imported, although you can find local pork, goat and chicken.

Seafood has a distinct and intense flavour here, most likely because it is served so fresh. Fish such as snapper, mahi-mahi (also known as dorado or dolphin), wahoo, flying fish and tuna are all available, as are crab, spiny lobster (in season September to April) and conch (same season). The result is that mealtimes can often be a delicious cornucopia of fragrances and flavours. Weekly street parties at Anse la Raye, Dennery and Vieux Fort are fun places to try local, seasonal seafood. Fishermen bring the freshest catch of the day, including huge lobsters, to be cooked on barbecues made from oil drums, where you can pick whatever you fancy for dining under the stars.

Breakfast is usually available from 7–10am, lunch noon–2pm and dinner 6–10pm. Some restaurant kitchens stay open until 11pm, particularly if there is a bar attached, but generally late-night dining is not common. Castries is not known for its nightlife, although there are lots of places for lunch catering to the office workers and cruise-ship visitors. The greatest concentration of restaurants is in the Rodney Bay area where most of the hotels are. These are of a good standard – some are excellent – and so varied that all tastes are accommodated. From beach bars to fine dining, there is a wide range for all budgets.

Breadfruit

The breadfruit was brought to the region in 1793 by Captain Bligh (of *Mutiny on the Bounty* fame) and its large round fruit was useful to provide enslaved people with carbohydrates and vitamins A, B and C.

WHAT TO EAT

Many of the foods the Indigenous communities grew and consumed are still around today, notably cassava, sweet potatoes, yam, corn, peppers, avocado, okra, peanuts, cashew nuts and pumpkin. Native Americans delighted in roasted corn,

Chicken roti

and today it remains a popular and healthy snack. Street vendors roast the corn on barbecues, often until it is black.

Cassava bread is a St Lucian staple, first enjoyed by the Native Americans and later the enslaved West Africans, who brought with them their own version of the bread. Served as an accompaniment to a main meal or as a filling snack, modern cassava bread comes in a variety of flavours from sweet or cherry to smoked herring.

The island's national dish is green fig and saltfish, a tasty meal of seasoned salt cod and small green bananas, known locally as a fig. Also worth a try is hearty pumpkin soup or callaloo soup made from the green leaf of the dasheen, a common root vegetable. The leaves have a spinach-like appearance and can also be cooked up with onions and saltfish.

Saltfish was first introduced to the Caribbean as an easy-to-store, inexpensive source of protein for enslaved people working the land and it was they who created imaginative ways to cook it.

Making the best of what was on offer and what they could afford has inspired generations of Caribbean cooks, so it is little wonder that menus include dishes made from almost every imaginable part of a pig or cow.

Pigs' tails are a local speciality, cooked in a juicy stew. Other stews include pepperpot – a combination of meats, vegetables and hot peppers with cassava juice – while souse bouillon contains salt beef cooked with a spicy mix of onions, beans, little dumplings and potatoes. Then there is cowheel soup and oxtail, chicken and beef, stewed, fried, baked or in mouthwatering curries.

The word 'provisions' on a menu indicates a variety of root or starchy vegetables, such as yams, sweet potatoes or tannia. Side dishes include breadfruit roasted or boiled, cut in slices or cubed in a salad, accras (spicy deep-fried fishcakes made with salt cod), cassava, dasheen, sweet potato, yam, green fig, plantain, lentils, plain rice and rice and peas. These can be green or dried pigeon peas, black eye, split peas or lentils. Christophene, another local vegetable, is often served baked in a cheese sauce. Bakes are a

MANGOES

Although there are more than 100 varieties of mango, just seven can be found in great numbers on St Lucia. Around 2,000 tons of the fruit are exported each year to as far afield as the UK. Of the seven common varieties only a few actually originate from St Lucia; they include the large juicy Cabishe, the Long and the Pa Louis mangoes. The sweet, orange-coloured Julie mango actually comes from Trinidad. Though closely associated with the region the mango, like the banana, is not indigenous. The fruit, be it sweet or tart, smooth or stringy in texture, can be juiced to produce a drink or made into ice cream or chutney.

Breakfast with a view

fried dough patty filled with fish or corned beef, a popular snack bought in most bakeries.

Roti, a flat unleavened bread wrap that contains a spicy meat, fish or vegetarian filling, is a filling lunch. Originating in Trinidad where it was developed by immigrants from India, the roti has spread up the island chain and is more popular than the sandwich.

The island's food is flavoursome because of the seasonings used, of which onions, garlic, lime, peppers, thyme, ginger, clove, cinnamon and nutmeg are the most common. You will find a bottle of hot pepper sauce – made from scotch bonnet pepper – on almost every table, but be careful when adding it to your food as the strength of the sauce can vary greatly from mild to fiery.

Fruits

Well known for its small sweet bananas, the island also produces tropical fruits, including guava, soursop (chirimoya, guanabana), mango (see box, page 106), papaya (paw paw), pineapple, orange, grapefruit, lime, passionfruit, tamarind, sapodilla (zapote), carambola (star fruit), sugar apple (custard apple, sweetsop) and coconut. Fruit is everywhere, made into juice, ice cream, pickles and chutneys. No surprise, then that hotels usually offer a wide range of fruits at their breakfast buffets.

Sweets and pastries

The region's love affair with sugar stems back to the seventeenth-century plantation era when St Lucia began its sugar industry. Those with a sweet tooth won't be disappointed with a choice of sweets and pastries as varied as tangy tamarind balls and coconut sugar cakes, cinnamon turnovers and banana bread. And don't forget the island fruit preserves such as guava jelly. Cocoa and

SMALL BUT SWEET

Bananas grown in the Windward Islands are smaller and (some say) sweeter than the larger fruit from elsewhere. Although you can find them in supermarkets in the northern hemisphere, you will notice that they are sweeter here, because they have been allowed to ripen longer on the plant. Bananas picked for export are ripened artificially, which affects the flavour. Unripe, green bananas, known as green fig, are cooked, much like plantains, which are also eaten in St Lucia. The island is closely associated with the banana, a dominant crop for decades until the late 1990s, when farmers were forced to begin diversifying crops. Bananas are grown by small-scale farmers, either organically or with the minimum of chemicals. The plant takes around 9–10 months to develop, and can propagate itself by producing suckers on its stem, which can then be planted to produce another plant.

chocolate are now firmly on the tourist trail, with several old cacao plantations around Soufrière having been renovated and opened for visitors with demonstrations of the bean-to-bar process. Not only can you eat and drink it, but you can be massaged with cocoa butter or defoliated with cocoa nibs. The possibilities are endless. So important has cocoa become, that August has been dedicated Cocoa Heritage Month.

Know your measures

In a rum shop, a 'flask' is a small, flat bottle holding enough for four people to share, maybe with a mixer; a 'nip' serves three, a 'half nip' serves two, while a 'shot' is an individual measure. A 'mix' is rum and falernum, a spiced syrup (alcoholic or non-alcoholic) from Barbados.

WHAT TO DRINK

Refreshing fruit juices abound, including orange, mango, pineapple, grapefruit, lime, guava and passionfruit. Unripe, green coconuts are full of refreshing, sterile water, sold by roadside vendors, who will hack off the top with a machete and provide you with a drinking straw. The water and jelly round the edge of the shell is full of potassium, magnesium and antioxidants. Tamarind is a bitter sweet drink made from the pulp around the seeds inside the pods (legumes) of the tamarind tree, and contains calcium as well as B vitamins. At Christmas it is traditional to make a bright red sorrel drink, naturally coloured by the petals of the sorrel flower and spiced with cinnamon, cloves, ginger and orange peel. St Lucians also drink a variety of herbal teas, often for medicinal reasons, and a knowledge of herbs and their uses is passed down through the generations. Cocoa tea is drunk at breakfast, but do not expect it to be like the commercial varieties of hot chocolate. Cocoa beans are dried, fermented and roasted before being ground and compacted into cocoa sticks or balls, often with spices such as cinnamon and nutmeg. These are then grated and added to hot water (or milk), sweetened to taste and served as cocoa tea.

Islanders are rightly proud of their rum. St Lucia Distillers produces a selection of dark and white rums at its factory in the Roseau Valley (see page 51). The dark rums include Bounty, most commonly used in cocktails and punches, TOZ Gold and Elements 8 Gold. Connoisseurs can try the extra-aged Admiral Rodney and Chairman's Reserve. Crystal is a white rum, used in cocktails, while Denros is a double strength 160° proof rum (good for rubbing on aching joints even if you can't drink it).

In the island rum shops (known as *cabawe*) rum is served straight up or on the rocks, but the uninitiated can enjoy theirs in a blend of tropical fruit juices or with other mixers. There are also ready-made rum punches such as Smugglers rum punch, spiced rum such as Kwèyòl Spiced Rum and rum-based liqueurs such as Crème la Caye, Nutz & Rum (a peanut blend) and Orange Bliss. There are some 20 blended, flavoured or unadulterated rum products in all. Less potent is the local beer: Piton. Brewed in Vieux Fort, it is a lager, best drunk very cold. A shandy is usually a mixture of beer and ginger ale, but a Piton shandy can be with lemon, sorrel or ginger.

Admire Petit Piton while supping a mojito

WHERE TO EAT

You will never be far from somewhere to eat, but the greatest concentration of restaurants is in Rodney Bay, where a week's holiday is not long enough to try them all. Below is a selection of restaurants, divided into three categories according to the price of a main course:

$$$ over US$30

$$ US$15–30

$ less than US$15

CASTRIES

Auberge Seraphine $$ *Vielle Bay, Pointe Seraphine; tel: 758-453 2073;* www.aubergeseraphine.com. A lovely place with an international menu, popular with business visitors and tourists. Overlooks the marina, best at twilight when you can watch the yachts, roosting egrets and departing cruise ships. Open daily for breakfast, lunch and dinner.

Caribbean Pirates $$$ *La Place Carenage; tel: 758-452 2543.* On the waterfront and popular with locals and the cruise-ship crowd alike, this stylish bar-restaurant serves nouvelle creole cuisine. Seafood is the speciality; try the shrimp roti. Open Mon–Sat for lunch and dinner, Sun only when cruise ships dock.

The Coal Pot $$$ *Vigie Marina; tel: 758-452 5566;* www.coalpotrestaurant.com. One of the island's oldest (and best) restaurants, *The Coal Pot* has been within the same family for over forty years and remains popular with locals. The cuisine is a fusion of French and creole, with choices like cognac-flavoured lobster bisque to start, followed by that day's catch: dorado, barracuda, calamari. On the water's edge, this is a perfect place for a special night out. Open Mon–Fri for lunch and dinner, Sat dinner only.

Pink Papaya Patio Restaurant $$ *Pointe Seraphine; tel: 758-453 6862;* www.facebook.com/PinkPapayaRestaurant. Located right by the cruise piers, *Pink*

Papaya serves tasty seafood and excellent pizzas fresh from its wood-fired oven. With an extensive wine list and delicious cocktails (don't miss the signature Pink Papaya), it's a top spot for a long lunch. Open Mon–Fri 11am–4pm. Food served 11.30am–3pm.

Pink Plantation House $$ *The Morne, Chef Harry Drive; tel: 758-452 5422;* www.pinkplantationstlucia.com. Up on the hill in lush gardens overlooking Castries harbour, the *Pink Plantation House* is tousled by a gentle breeze. Tables are scattered across a veranda with glorious views; the food is varied, tasty and plentiful; the service attentive and friendly. Owned by a ceramicist; you can see her workshop and buy her ceramics. Reservations advised. Open Mon–Thurs 11.30am–3pm, Fri 11.30am–9pm, Sun 9am–noon.

RODNEY BAY AND NORTH

Big Chef $$$ *Reduit Drive, Rodney Bay; tel: 758-450 0210;* www.bigchef-steakhouse.com. Popular, busy and atmospheric, this is the place to come for tender, aged Angus beef steaks and a variety of seafood and fish, paired with excellent international wines. Live music on Tues and Sat. Dinner served from 5pm Tues to Sat, Sun brunch from noon.

Blue Monkey Café $ *JQ Mall, Rodney Bay; tel: 758-4854600.* A great place to pick up coffee or fresh juice, and also good for light bites. Filling breakfasts include stuffed toasted baguettes or burger buns, which will set you up for the day. For lunch try a hearty soup, roti or tasty salad. Outdoor seating with umbrellas for shade. Open Mon–Fri 8am–4.30pm, Sat 8am–4pm.

The Cliff at Cap $$$ *Cap Maison, Smugglers Cove Drive, Cap Estate; tel: 758-457 8681;* www.thecliffatcap.com. Nouveau French Caribbean fusion cuisine in a gorgeous clifftop setting overlooking the sea. On a clear day, views stretch all the way to Martinique. Arrive for sundowners while it's still light; ask for a table on the wooden deck at the base of the cliffs. You don't have to be a guest at *Cap Maison* to eat here, which is lucky as this is one of the island's best places to dine. Smart but friendly spot, with incredible attention to detail; the fine-dining experience is as enjoyable as the vistas. Try the roast jerk pork belly with caramelized plantain. Lunch served noon–2.30pm, dinner 6–10pm.

Flavours of the Grill $$ *Marie Therese St, Gros Islet; tel: 758-284 7906.* A modest restaurant set in a traditional wooden cottage painted blue, pink and lime green, with tables spilling out onto the veranda. Authentic, inexpensive Caribbean classics include grilled fish, chicken, curried goat and sometimes lobster, served with local side dishes such as rice and peas. Be sure to save room for the banana rum pudding. If you're dining on a Friday, enjoy the weekly barbecue then head to the main drag of Gros Islet afterwards for a very lively street party. Open Mon–Thurs, Fri noon–1am, Sat noon–10pm. Reservations advised.

Jambe de Bois $ *Pigeon Island National Landmark; tel: 758-452 0321.* Seafront cafe serving up St Lucian specialities in the park. A pleasant place to take a break after hiking up the hill, to sit and watch the boating activity in the bay, whether for drinks, lunch or dinner. Not a place to go if you are in a rush; the pace is unhurried. With good snorkelling just offshore, you could make a day of it. Open for lunch and dinner.

Jacques Waterfront Dining (Froggie Jacques) $$$ *Rodney Bay Village; tel: 758-458 1900;* www.jacquesrestaurant.com. A warm and personal bar and restaurant that's big on good (if slightly overpriced) food and small on overdressed pomp. Lovely setting at the end of Reduit Beach by the entrance to the marina, offering waterfront dining. A long-established restaurant dishing up fusion French and Caribbean food, although it has relocated since the original Vigie building burned down. Emphasis is on hearty dishes and home-smoked fish, but vegetarians are well catered for and special requests welcome. Open daily noon–3pm and 6–10pm.

Key Largo Italian $$ *Key Largo Way, Rodney Bay; tel: 758-452 0282;* www.keylargoitalianslu.com. Boasting St Lucia's first wood-fired pizza oven, this family-friendly favourite has been serving authentic Italian food since 1989. While the pizzas are the main draw, classics like chicken Milanese and spaghetti meatballs are hearty and tasty, with local seafood well represented in the spaghetti *frutti di mare*. Open 11.30am–10.30pm, closed Mon. Happy hour 5.30–6.30pm.

The Naked Fisherman $$ *Cap Maison Resort & Spa, Smugglers Cove, Cap Estate; tel: 758-457 8694;* www.nakedfishermanstlucia.com. From the team behind *Cap Maison*, this beach bar and grill is a simple, unpretentious haunt set on a delightful cove. With 92 steps down to the beach, people tend to stay a while before climbing back up again. The food is good and varied (though pricey), from gourmet burgers and salads to seafood plates for lunch, with extra meat dishes for supper. Standouts include crab claws in a ginger and chilli sauce, jerk pork and chicken roti, though you can't go wrong with catch of the day, usually served with sweet potato fries and curried pumpkin. Open daily, lunch 12.30pm–4pm, dinner Thurs–Sat 6–9.30pm.

Razmataz $$ *Rodney Bay, opposite the Royal St Lucian Hotel; tel: 758-452 9800;* www.razmatazrestaurant.com. Long-established tandoori restaurant helmed by a Nepalese chef. Lots of flavoursome dishes and generous portions. Try the Kerala Colada cocktail – an aromatic hit of coconut cream, ginger, rum, pineapple and cinnamon. Open-air dining with Indian decor and tables on covered veranda. Happy hour 5–7pm with light bites at the bar. Open 5–11pm, closed Tues.

Spice of India $$$ *Bay Walk Mall, Rodney Bay Village; tel: 758-458 4243;* www.spiceofindiastlucia.com. Sophisticated, scrumptious Indian food prepared by chefs from India with imported ingredients, while taking advantage of local delicacies like crab and shrimp. Good meat dishes, and lots of tasty options for vegetarians too. Friendly and hospitable service; a very popular spot so reservations advised. Open daily noon–3.45pm and 6pm onwards (closed Mon lunch).

Ti Bananne Caribbean Bistro and Bar $$ *Coco Palm resort, Gros Islet; tel: 758-4562800*. Located within the *Coco Palm Resort*, the family-owned, family-run *Ti Bananne* offers island favourites (coconut curry, spiced chicken, ginger-glazed snapper) alongside excellent artisanal pizza. The rum menu is impressive, too. Open noon–8pm.

Wingz-N-Tingz $ *Seagrape Ave, Rodney Bay; tel: 758-451 8200;* email wingzntingz@hotmail.com. A good place to come for fast food, particularly the marinated chicken wings cooked on the barbecue with a variety of sauces. There are other dishes, though, such as catch of the day; and the green banana salad should be tried. Excellent fresh juices or a cold Piton beer to wash it down. Occasional live music. Open lunch and dinner.

MARIGOT BAY

Hurricane Hole Bar and Restaurant $$ *Marigot Bay Marina Village.* Perched right on the water overlooking La Bas beach, *Hurricane Hole* is the perfect place to linger over happy-hour cocktails while watching the sun sink into the sea. As for the food, take your pick from thin-crust pizzas, fresh calamari, crispy conch fritters and chicken wings, or order from sister restaurant *Chateau Mygo*'s menu for fancy food in a more laidback setting. Open daily for lunch and dinner.

SOUFRIÈRE AND ENVIRONS

The Beacon $ *Columbette, Soufrière; tel: 758-286 9659;* www.thebeaconrestaurant.restaurantsnapshot.com. On the main road from the north to Soufrière and a convenient place to stop for lunch while on an island tour, *The Beacon* can be busy with coach parties. Perched up high, it has a fantastic view over the town and bay, to the Pitons beyond. Lunch is usually a set-price buffet of local food; all tasty and well prepared. Its peaceful maranatha garden is planted with a beautiful display of colourful tropical plants. Open lunch and dinner.

Big Yard $ *Sir Darnley Alexander St, Soufrière.* Serving generous portions of hearty Creole dishes at great prices, *Big Yard* has a friendly laidback vibe. Whether you go for the saltfish, barbecue chicken, or stewed pork, your dish will come with tonnes of tasty provisions. The mac and cheese is heavenly. Open daily 10am–10pm.

Boucan Restaurant & Bar $$$ *Hotel Chocolat, Rabot Estate; tel: 758-457 1624;* www.hotelchocolat.com. The big-hitting restaurant of *Hotel Chocolat* certainly has the 'wow' factor. *Boucan* is set on a working cocoa plantation where the menu for both sweet and savoury dishes and drinks is rooted in cocoa. Recipes are inventive but subtle, using locally sourced, seasonal ingredients; think bread dipped into a chocolate-infused vinaigrette, a citrus salad drizzled with a white chocolate dressing, fillet of pork with a cocoa and herb crust. Perched high up with spectacular views of the Pitons, the minimalist design allows you to concentrate on the gourmet food or your sunset cocktail. Open daily for breakfast, lunch, dinner or just drinks.

The Creole Pot at Fond Doux Eco Resort $$$ *Fond Deux Plantation, Soufrière; tel: 758-731 3090;* www.fonddouxresort.com. Organic fruits and vegetables from the estate are used to create incredible St Lucian creole cuisine in a lush tropical setting – the plantation gardens teem with dazzling birds and blooms. Consider booking a chocolate heritage tour of the plantation and finishing it up with lunch here. Open for lunch.

Dasheene $$$ *Ladera Resort; tel: 758-459 6600;* www.ladera.com. Award-winning restaurant with innovative dishes using fresh local ingredients. From the dining terrace, breathtaking views take in the Pitons, the forested slopes of the southwest of the island and the sea. The menu is a mix of international and creole dishes – try the sautéed shrimp with peppers, sweet potato and breadfruit chips. Live music at dinner. Open for breakfast, lunch, dinner & Sun brunch.

Fedo's $ *New Development, Soufrière; tel: 758-459 5220.* In the residential area, off the road which leads to the Botanical Gardens. Ask locally for directions, and look for a blue-and-white painted house. Local lunches, everything fresh, tasty, filling and cheap. A good place to try island home cooking. Open for lunch Mon–Sat.

Hummingbird $$ *Hummingbird Beach Resort, Soufrière; tel: 758-459 7232.* A pleasant spot by the sea, with a view of the Pitons across Soufrière Bay. As its name suggests, there are hummingbirds aplenty here, too. Good for a meal or just drinks to watch the sunset from the *Lifeline Bar*. Creole specialities and the fish and seafood are fresh and tasty. Open for lunch and dinner.

Jade Mountain $$$ *Jade Mountain, Soufrière; tel: 758-459 4000;* www.jademountainstlucia.com. Luxury hotel restaurant, reservations required. Lunch is the better option because you can enjoy the spectacular view of the Pitons from the restaurant perched on top of this futuristic resort; plus it is a much cheaper option. Stay until sunset and leave when it gets dark. Dinner is a set menu and expensive.

The Mango Tree $$ *Stonefield Estate Resort, Soufrière; tel: 758-459 7037;* www.stonefieldresort.com. On the hillside with views of Petit Piton, *The Mango Tree* exudes a lovely, relaxed atmosphere. The menu is crammed with local dishes, such as spicy roti, made using homegrown organic produce. Vegan options available. Barbecue and entertainment on Thurs, steel pan on Sat. Open daily 7.30am–10pm.

Martha's Tables $ *Jalousie Rd, Soufrière; tel: 758-459 7270;* www.marthastables.com. Set in the shadow of Petit Piton, this is a great place to stop for lunch if you're in the area – and also worth making a journey to. The restaurant may appear unassuming, but this is St Lucian cooking at its best – chef Martha serves homemade creole dishes to patrons on the terrace of her home. Choose your main – grilled chicken breast, shrimp, fishcakes, fish – and expect an abundance of sides plonked down beside your dish: plantains, rice and beans, macaroni cheese, potato salad, spicy creole sauce. With any luck, the warm-spiced St Lucian pepper pot will on the menu when you visit. Open Mon–Fri 11.30am–3pm.

Orlando's $$ *Cemetery Rd, Fond Bernier, Soufrière; tel: 758-572 6613.* Small, cosy and intimate, this is something of a Soufrière institution – and is by far the the best place to eat in town. *Orlando's* serves up delectable gourmet creole meals, tasting menus and simpler fare for lunch, using ingredients bought fresh that day in Soufrière market. Try the grilled trigger fish and plantain chips, followed by baked banana filled with guava and ice cream. Excellent service from warm and welcoming staff. Open Tues–Sun from 6pm, also lunch from noon with reservation.

VIEUX FORT AND SOUTH COAST

The Reef Beach Café $$ *Anse De Sables; tel: 758-454 3418;* www.slucia.com/reef. Casual beach café with Caribbean fare such as saltfish, bakes, seafood salad and T-bone steak; there is also an à la carte menu available for dinner. Internet access and wheelchair access. Open for lunch and dinner.

EAST COAST

Whispering Palm $$ *Fox Grove Inn, Mon Repos; tel: 758-455 3271;* www.foxgroveinn.com. A good lunch stop if touring this side of the island. Eat indoors or outside on the balcony for lovely views down to the east coast. Open daily for breakfast, lunch and dinner.

TRAVEL ESSENTIALS

PRACTICAL INFORMATION

A

ACCOMMODATION

While St Lucia has a reputation for expensive all-inclusive accommodation, the island has a pretty big range of places to stay, with something for every budget, from large all-inclusive resorts and luxury boutique hotels to small, intimate inns and basic bed and breakfasts. Most of the resorts are in the north, the drier end of the island, which is where you also find a bigger choice of restaurants and bars for convenient nightlife around Rodney Bay. While the Soufrière area has some very classy places to stay – designers have made the most of the dramatic landscape to provide stunning views of the Pitons from luxurious rooms – it also boasts attractive, affordable accommodation options for travellers on a budget, or for those who want to see St Lucia beyond the confines of a resort.

Basic bed and breakfasts run by St Lucians who open up their homes to visitors are popular with budget-conscious travellers who don't mind staying off the beaten track and don't need the creature comforts offered by the upmarket resorts. Local hosts will also be able to point you in the direction of little-known sights and the best places to enjoy authentic creole cuisine. If you are staying in a rural area or far from reliable public transport links you are best advised to rent a sturdy vehicle, or seek out a guide, because taxi fares can mount up.

Another option is renting a self-catering apartment or villa, which are available mainly in the northern Cap Estate area, with a handful of options elsewhere. Rates often include housekeeping and cooking services. For rentals, contact Blue Sky Luxury (Castries tel: 758/450-8240, www.blueskyluxurystlucia.com), Oliver's Travels (www.oliverstravels.com/caribbean/st-lucia) or Rental Escapes (www.rentalescapes.com).

AIRPORTS

Long-distance scheduled and charter flights, such as trans-Atlantic flights, fly in to **Hewanorra International Airport** (UVF) at Vieux Fort in the south,

67km (42 miles) from Castries. If you are staying at a hotel in the far north of the island be prepared for a scenic journey of up to two hours to get to your destination. Another, smaller airport, the **George F.L. Charles Airport** (SLU) is located at Vigie, on the outskirts of Castries, which receives inter-island flights. Airlines using the Vigie airport include LIAT, Air Caraïbes, Winair and American Eagle. Daily arrivals and departure information can be found on www.slaspa.com. There is a helicopter shuttle from Hewanorra to George F.L. Charles Airport (**St Lucia Helicopters Ltd**, tel: 453 6950; www.stluciahelicopters.com). It is not a cheap option but it does cut travelling time right down to 10 minutes for the trip between the two airports.

B

BICYCLE RENTAL

St Lucia is not easy for cyclists. The roads are steep, twisty and potholed, and traffic moves fast, often on the wrong side of the road. Watch out for storm drains. Bikes and scooters can be rented from **Pirate Rentals** (Rodney Bay, tel: 758-724 5111). Off-road cycling for tourists is offered by **Bike St Lucia** (tel: 758-457 1400, www.bikestlucia.com), on trails at Anse Mamin Plantation, near Soufrière, and by **Palm Services Rainforest Cycling Adventure** (tel: 758-458 0908, www.adventuretoursstlucia.com), at Errard Plantation on the east coast.

BUDGETING FOR YOUR TRIP

Getting to St Lucia. The cheapest direct scheduled return fares from London in high season are around £600 with either TUI, British Airways or Virgin Atlantic, although good-value deals including accommodation as well as flights are available if you prefer a package holiday.

Accommodation. High season is mid-December to mid-April, when prices are at their highest. Substantial discounts can be found at other times of the year, particularly during hurricane season. The cheapest accommodation is in self-catering apartments, which will cost US$30–50 a night depending on location and time of year. The most expensive rooms come with a spectacular view of the Pitons and cost over US$1,000 a night. There are plenty of options in between, but be mindful of a value-added tax of 10 percent, and a service charge of 10 percent. In some cases, quoted prices include these charges, but check to be sure.

An addition, as of 1 December 2020, St Lucia introduced a Tourism Levy on accommodation, with guests charged $3 or $6 (US) per person, per night, depending on whether their room rate is below or above $120. Guests aged 15–17 are subject to 50 percent of the levy, with no fee for under-12s. In the words of tourism minister Dominic Fedee, this was brought in to "ensure that the Saint Lucia Tourism Authority (SLTA) is self-sustainable".

Meals. If you are self-catering, a visit to the market will reveal a wealth of seasonal tropical fruits and vegetables at a fraction of the price you would typically pay at home. You can also eat economically at local stalls in the Castries market to sample traditional dishes or at laidback bars and family restaurants around the island. Prices in international-style restaurants in popular tourist areas or in hotels are much higher at around US$30–40 for a main course. Rum and rum-based cocktails are relatively cheap, but wine or imported spirits are expensive.

Local transport. Bus transport is cheap and easy to use. Short journeys cost as little as EC$2.50 (US$1), rising to a maximum of EC$8 (US$3) from one end of the island to the other. However, they do not always go where you want nor when, so taxi or car hire may be a better option, depending on what you want to do. A taxi from Castries to Gros Islet costs US$30 and from Hewanorra Airport to Rodney Bay US$100. A day's tour of the island is about US$200–250, depending on how far you go and for how long. Fares are set by the Government but you should always verify it in advance and check in which currency it is quoted.

Incidentals. Excursions are likely to be your biggest expense. A two-hour sunset cruise costs upwards of US$75 per person, including drinks, while a day sail including lunch, land tours and snorkelling is around US$130. Whale-watching boat tours are US$60–80 for three hours. Popular land-based activities such as segway tours around Rodney Bay start from US$85, while zip-lining ranges from US$50–100, depending on which option you choose.

C

CAR HIRE

In St Lucia you drive on the left. Visiting drivers must be over 25 years old and under 65, and should possess an international driver's licence (with an official stamp from the Immigration Department) or obtain a temporary driving permit, which is valid for three months, by presenting a current driving licence at the main police station (Bridge Street, Castries). The car rental company can also process a temporary permit, for which there is a charge of US$21 (EC$54). The wearing of seat belts is compulsory.

There is a choice of car-rental companies with offices at the airports and in many resorts. Most will deliver the vehicle to your hotel and collect it at the end of the rental period. Daily rental rates are around US$50 for a car and US$75 for a SUV, but there is a 15 percent tax added to everything. It can be cheaper to rent in advance, and in high season this is more reliable. The major agents are: **Sixt**, tel: +33 1 44 38 55 55, www.sixt.co.uk/car-hire/st-lucia; **Hertz**, tel: 758-452 0679; www.hertzcaribbean.com; **Drive-A-Matic**, tel: 758-452 0544, www.driveamatic.com.

CLIMATE

St Lucia has a tropical, humid climate with warm sunshine most of the year, cooled by northeastern trade winds. During the tourist high season (December to April) temperatures can reach a sizzling 28–31°C (82–88°F), accompanied by a light breeze and short showers. The hottest months are June to August, while December and January are the coolest, when night and early morning temperatures can plummet to 21°C (69°F). It is several degrees cooler in the rainforest and mountain villages, and colder still high up on the mountain peaks.

The rainy season runs from June to the end of November and is characterized by sporadic heavy showers. The annual rainfall can be up to three times higher in the mountains in the south (3,450mm/136 inches) than on the coast in the north (1,500mm/59 inches).

The hurricane season is generally between June and November, coinciding with the rainy season. Storms are the most damaging weather phenomenon in the Caribbean, but St Lucia's marinas and sheltered harbours on the Leeward (Caribbean) coast are popular with the sailing fraternity. However, the steep hilly terrain means St Lucia is particularly susceptible to mudslides caused by torrential downpours of rain, which often lead to casualties and huge farming losses.

	J	F	M	A	M	J	J	A	S	O	N	D
ºC	26	25	26	27	28	28	28	28	28	28	27	26
ºF	79	77	79	81	82	82	82	82	82	82	81	79

CLOTHING

Stick to cool and comfortable attire in the heat. Wearing skimpy shorts, skirts or beachwear while sightseeing and shopping in town is considered inappropriate. Most restaurants prefer their guests to dress elegantly casual, however some of the more upmarket establishments may require men to wear a jacket and occasionally a tie.

In winter the evenings can be quite chilly, as can the air-conditioning, so it's best to carry a light cardigan or wrap with you; don't forget to take a lightweight umbrella or raincoat to protect you from brief showers during the rainy season.

CRIME AND SAFETY

St Lucia is a relatively safe island but crime, especially petty theft, certainly exists. By all means relax while on holiday but don't leave home without your common sense. Keep an eye on personal possessions and important documents when wandering in the markets and the busy resort areas; keep your money in a safe place, and leave your expensive jewellery at home or in the hotel safe. If you are renting a car keep valuables out of sight as you would at home, preferably locked in the boot, and don't offer lifts to strangers. Avoid the beaches and out-of-the-way sidestreets after dark.

It is likely that you will be approached by local vendors offering anything from hair braiding to crafts and a variety of souvenirs on the beach and at popular tourist attractions. If you are genuinely interested in what's on offer, feel free to haggle for an agreeable price, but don't waste people's time; this is their livelihood. A firm but polite "no, thank you" is usually sufficient to deter any further advances.

CULTURE

St Lucian culture is archetypal Caribbean: a syncretic amalgamation of the customs, languages and religions of the island's French and British colonizers, and of the enslaved African people they brought over the Atlantic. Today's population of 165,000 is of predominantly African origin, and some seventy percent are Roman Catholic, with the remainder largely made up of Protestants (Anglican, Baptist and Pentecostal), as well as a small number of Rastafarians. Though Christian hymns are sung boisterously enough to raise the church roofs each Sunday, St Lucia is a society in which esoteric African traditions of magic and spiritualism are very much alive. Carnival is the best example of this fusion of Christian and African beliefs: even though the festival originated as a pre-Lenten celebration (it's now held in July), one of the costume parade's stock characters is the distinctly non-Christian moko jumbie, a wildly attired figure on stilts representing the spirit world.

Language is another aspect that shows African influence. Though African languages were suppressed as soon as enslaved people arrived on the island, French planters still needed to communicate with their workers, and gradually the common language of St Lucian Creole (Kwéyòl) – also called Patois – evolved, heavily laced with French, West African dialects and more recently, with smatterings of English.

Though English became St Lucia's official language in 1842, Creole is still spoken widely throughout the island, on the radio, in parliament, and many rural St Lucians speak only Creole until they start primary school, where they learn English for the first time.

D

DRIVING

Hiring a car gives you the greatest flexibility when driving around St Lucia, but it is more relaxing to hire a driver/guide for an island tour. You can negotiate an itinerary, you don't have to worry about navigating unfamiliar, twisty mountain roads or losing your way and you will receive a wealth of information about the island.

Road conditions. The government has invested heavily in road improvements in recent years, and generally major roads and bridges are in good condition. However, rural roads can be potholed and may require a 4WD vehicle. In the rainy season there are often landslides which can block or damage roads, so if there has been a storm you should seek local advice, particularly before driving down the west coast. Avoid driving after dark; street lighting can be poor and oncoming vehicles often do not dip their headlights.

Rules and regulations. Driving is on the left, as in the UK, although the steering wheel may be on either side. At roundabouts give way to traffic already on the circle coming from your right. Seat belts are compulsory for all passengers. The speed limit is 30mph on highways, 15mph in towns, although this is widely disregarded.

Fuel costs. Filling stations are open from around 6.30–7am and stay open until about 8pm, Mon–Sat. A few open on Sun in the afternoon. Prices are set by the government in line with international prices.

E

ELECTRICITY

220 volts, 50 cycles AC and 110 volts, 60 cycles AC.

EMBASSIES AND CONSULATES

British High Commission, 2nd floor Francis Compton Building, Waterfront, Castries, tel: 758-452 2484; email: britishhc@candw.lc

US Embassy, located in Barbados, at Wildey Business Park, Barbados, tel: (246) 227-4000; https://bb.usembassy.gov/embassy/bridgetown.

EMERGENCIES

The emergency number for Police, Fire and Ambulance is **911**.

GETTING THERE

Air travel. The frequency of flights varies according to the season and many charter flights stop in the summer months and in the hurricane season. Schedules usually change mid-April. There are frequent flights from London Gatwick with both Virgin Atlantic and British Airways. TUI also flies weekly from Gatwick. From the US, there are direct flights from JFK New York and Boston with Jet Blue, from Miami with American Airlines, from Charlotte and Philadelphia with US Airways and from Atlanta and New York with Delta. Air Canada, Air Transat, Sunwing and WestJet fly from Toronto, Canada. Air Canada flies from Montréal. There are lots of flights connecting St Lucia with other islands in the Caribbean if you want to island-hop with a regional airline, such as Air Caraïbes, LIAT, Caribbean Airlines or American Eagle.

By sea. L'Express des Iles has a high-speed catamaran car ferry service linking St Lucia with Dominica and the French islands of Martinique, Guadeloupe, Les Saintes and Marie Galante, usually crossing three times a week. Travelling time is short enough to justify hopping over to a neighbouring island for a day or even a weekend, but remember that this is an international crossing and you should take your passport. Avoid island-hopping on the day you are leaving St Lucia because there is no guarantee that your ferry will return in time for you to make an airline connection. The agent in St Lucia, **Cox & Company Ltd**, has an office located at the ferry terminal on La Toc Road in Castries (Mon–Fri 8am–6pm, tel: 456 5022/23/24, www.express-des-iles.com). St Lucia is a popular port of call for cruise ships starting from Florida, San Juan, Puerto Rico and Barbados. The port of entry is Castries and the view across the glittering bay as the ship approaches the island is absolutely stunning. Cruise ships dock at

Pointe Seraphine or Place Carenage, either side of Castries harbour, and there is duty-free shopping at both locations.

GUIDES AND TOURS

There are lots of tours available on land and by sea, half or whole day, for which your hotel or the Tourist Board will have details, or you can negotiate a tour with a taxi driver, most of whom make excellent guides. **Sun Tours Caribbean** (tel: 758-456 9100, www.suntourscaribbean.com) offers a full range of tours and excursions for cruise-ship passengers and people staying on the island. The **St Lucia National Trust** (tel: 758-452 5005, www.slunatrust.org) and its affiliate, **Eco-South Tours** (tel: 758-454 5014, ecosouthtoursinc@gmail.com) offer nature tours of the Maria Islands and other natural attractions in the southeast.

H

HEALTH AND MEDICAL CARE

St Lucia's main public medical facility is the Owen King European Union (OKEU) Hospital (tel: 758-458 6500). Located off Millennium Highway in Castries, it opened in March 2020 and is believed to be the EU's largest investment in the Caribbean.

Another major public facility, Victoria Hospital (tel: 758-452 2421), is based near the ferry terminal in Castries, while private hospitals include St Jude's Hospital in Vieux Fort (tel: 758-454 6041) and the small Tapion Hospital in the south of Castries (tel: 758-459 2000), both having emergency services available to visitors. Elsewhere, there are medical centres and clinics in Soufrière (tel: 758-459 7258/5001) and Dennery (tel: 758-453 3310).

LANGUAGE

Although St Lucia has been a British territory since 1814 and the official language is English, FrenchCreole (Kwéyòl) is spoken by more than 90 percent of people in informal arenas and, due to a drive to preserve and promote Creole traditions, is increasingly used in official circles as well. See page 13.

LGBTQ+ TRAVELLERS

Homosexual acts are legal for women but illegal for men, with penalties of up to ten years in prison. St Lucian society is conservative and religious and there have been violent homophobic attacks on gay St Lucians. There is no overtly gay scene, although many bars, restaurants and some resorts are gay-friendly where tourists are concerned. You are advised to be discreet with your partner, with no overt displays of affection in public places.

M

MAPS

There are several maps of the island distributed free in hotels and restaurants as well as in the tourist-information booths and car-hire companies. These are generally adequate for getting around the island on main roads and have local attractions clearly marked. Skyviews (www.skyviews.com) is one of the best, funded by advertising. For a more detailed topographical map, there is the Ordnance Survey map of St Lucia, dating from 1991, while the best road map is the Gizi Map, 2008.

MEDIA

St Lucia's newspapers can be read in print or online: *The Star*, www.stluciastar.com; *The Voice*, www.thevoiceslu.com; *The St Lucia Mirror*, www.stluciamirroronline.org. Online-only newspapers include *St Lucia Times*, www.stluciatimes.com and *St Lucia News Online*, www.stlucianewsonline.com. Monthly magazine *Tropical Traveller* (www.facebook.com/tropicaltraveller) promotes restaurants and gives information about upcoming events, while a biannual magazine, *Visions of St Lucia*, has listings and features about the island's attractions. Both are distributed through hotels. There are nine local television channels, including Choice39 TV and DBS. St Lucia also receives a host of programmes from the US via satellite. The island has 13 radio stations, including

Radio St Lucia, Radio 100 Helen FM, Radio Caribbean International and Hot FM, which broadcast local news and music.

MONEY

Currency. The official currency of St Lucia is the Eastern Caribbean dollar (EC$), which is pegged to the US dollar. The US dollar and all major credit cards and travellers' cheques are accepted in most places, including restaurants and shops, especially in the resort areas. EC dollars are produced in denominations of $100, $50, $20, $10 and $5 notes and $1, 25¢, 10¢, 5¢, 2¢ and 1¢ coins.

Currency exchange. There are foreign-exchange and banking facilities located in Castries, Rodney Bay, Vieux Fort, Soufrière and at Hewanorra International Airport, which usually opens at 12.30pm and only closes when the last flight leaves.

Credit cards. Large hotels, shops and restaurants accept credit cards, but bars and small businesses operate in cash. Banks have ATMs and accept all major international credit and debit cards.

OPENING TIMES

Banks are generally open Monday to Thursday 8am–2pm, and until 5pm on Friday, while in Rodney Bay they are open on Saturday until noon. Government offices open 8.30am–4pm, but close for lunch 12.30–1.30pm. Shops open Mon–Fri 8am–5pm and on Saturday until 12.30pm. Supermarkets operate extended opening hours.

POLICE

The main police station is located on Bridge Street, Castries (tel: 758-452 2854). In Rodney Bay the police station is beside the St Lucia Yacht Club on Reduit Beach Avenue (tel: 758-456 4061).

POST OFFICES

The main post office in the capital, Castries, is located on Bridge Street; Rodney Bay Mall and Gablewoods Mall have post office counters. There are small post offices in most towns, generally they are open Mon–Fri 8.30am–4.30pm.

PUBLIC HOLIDAYS

1 January: New Year's Day
2 January: New Year's Holiday
22 February: Independence Day
March/April: Easter
1 May: Labour Day; Whitsun (variable); Corpus Christi (variable)
1 August: Emancipation Day
1 October: Thanksgiving
13 December: National Day
25 December: Christmas Day
26 December: Boxing Day

T

TELEPHONES

If you plan to use your mobile a lot when you're away from wi-fi access, you could consider getting hold of a local pre-paid SIM card from one of the two network providers – Digicel or FLOW. Both providers have offices in Rodney Bay and Castries.

The international country code for St Lucia is **758**.

TIME ZONES

Four hours behind Greenwich Mean Time in the winter, five hours when Daylight Saving Time applies.

TIPPING

Be prepared to pay a 10 percent service charge and 10 percent government tax on all goods and services supplied by hotels and restaurants. In particular most restaurants and hotels will often automatically add a 10–15percent service charge to your bill, so no further gratuity is necessary unless you would like to tip an especially attentive waiter or another member of staff.

Where service is not included, a tip of 10–20 percent is usually appropriate. Porters, chambermaids and taxi drivers typically expect a tip, and you'll want to tip nature guides who often go above and beyond to find you that rare bird.

TOILETS

Toilets can be found in shopping malls, the cruise-ship complexes, tourist sites, hotels and restaurants. A few ranger stations in the forest have facilities, but they're few and far between, so take opportunities as they arise. The same goes if you're travelling through small villages.

TOURIST INFORMATION

The St Lucia Tourist Board's website is www.stlucia.org. The Tourist Board's administrative office is in Castries (PO Box 221, Sureline Building, Vide Bouteille, Castries, tel: 758-452 4094), but there are information booths at Hewanorra and George F.L. Charles airports, Pointe Seraphine and Place Carenage seaports in Castries.

Canada: 60 St. Clair Avenue East, Suite 909, Toronto, Ontario M4T 1N5, tel: (416) 362 4242

UK: 1 Collingham Gardens, London SW5 0HW, tel: 020 7341 7005

USA: 800 Second Avenue, 9th Floor, Suite 910, New York, NY 10017, tel: (212) 867 2951/2950

TRANSPORT

Buses. The public bus system in St Lucia operates from early in the morning until early evening. It is safe to say that more buses run in the morning and that the frequency tends to tail off after the end of the working day. Castries and Vieux Fort have the best services, but the more remote rural areas aren't always as well served. If you go to Soufrière by bus, it is usually quicker and easier to return via Vieux Fort, where there are better connections.

Buses can be distinguished from other minibuses by their licence plates, which begin with the letter M. The bus routes are zoned and priced accordingly, so a short hop costs EC$1.50, while a longer trip from Castries to Soufrière costs EC$8; note that you must have the exact fare. In Castries, buses for the north of the island leave from a terminus behind the market on Darling Road; buses for Anse la Raye and the west coast road leave from the south side of the market; buses for Dennery and Vieux Fort leave from Hospital Road by the river.

If you do travel on the bus, you'll hear people call out "one stop" when they want to get off. If you're not sure of the route and when to call out, ask the driver to let you know when you reach your destination.

Taxis. Taxis are available in the form of a saloon vehicle or a minivan that can accommodate a small group. They are plentiful at the airports, in the resort areas at hotels, at shopping malls and in town at the official stands. Look for the TX licence plate. Taxis are not metered because fares are fixed and the majority of drivers tend to stick to the published rates. However, it's always best to check the fare before setting off, and make sure you are being quoted in EC dollars.

A taxi is the obvious choice for the most convenient hotel transfer to and from the airport, unless your hotel offers a shuttle service. You can also arrange for a taxi driver/guide to take you on an island tour, on a shopping trip, or on an excursion to the Friday Night Fish Fry at Anse La Raye and the Jump-up at Gros Islet. Reliable and knowledgeable local drivers are affiliated to the following:

Rodney Bay: North Lime Taxi Association, Rodney Bay, tel: 758-452 8562, email: nltaxi@hotmail.com

Soufrière: Marc's Taxi Service and Tours, Waterfront, Soufrière, tel: 758-721 6469, www.marcstaxiservice.business.site.

TRAVELLERS WITH DISABILITIES

Facilities for visitors with disabilities are few, although some of the newer and larger hotels and resorts will be better equipped. In Castries and elsewhere the curbs and pavements can be high and difficult for wheelchair-users and the physically challenged to negotiate, but there are many accessible visitor attractions on the island. Check in advance that your hotel has the accessible facilities that you require and that the places you want to visit can accommodate you.

V

VISAS AND ENTRY REQUIREMENTS

Passports are required for entry to St Lucia, except for British, French, Canadian and US citizens on short visits (weekend to one week) holding return tickets. US citizens do, however, need a passport for re-entry into the US, and passports are highly recommended for ease of access into St Lucia for everyone. For visa requirements, other information and updates, see www.stlucia.gov.lc.

W

WEBSITES AND INTERNET ACCESS

www.stlucia.org The official St Lucia tourist site with information on how to get there, where to stay, how to get around and what to do.
www.gov.uk/foreign-travel-advice/st-lucia Travel advice from the British Foreign and Commonwealth Office, including safety, security and health alerts. US travellers should search for St Lucia on this site: www.travel.state.gov.
www.slunatrust.org The St Lucia National Trust has a number of protected sites, details of which are on this website.
www.forestryeeunit.blogspot.co.uk The Forestry Department maintains the forest trails and protects wildlife on St Lucia. This blog by the Environmental Education Unit contains news and information, as well as contact details for all the trails.

Resorts, hotels and guesthouses will almost certainly offer free wi-fi, though it's best to double-check if this is essential during your visit. St Lucia also has a number of free wi-fi zones in Castries Constitution Park, Vieux-Fort, Micoud, Canaries and Dennery. Many café, bars and restaurants offer free wi-fi access, too.

WHERE TO STAY

People who stay in Castries tend to be business travellers who need to be in the city, or visitors planning to take a ferry to neighbouring islands the next day. The north of the island is traditionally the place for beach resorts and package holidays, with a wide range of restaurants in and around Rodney Bay, which is also a magnet for those on yachts in search of a good marina. The southwest coast wrapping around Soufrière is the most beautiful part of the island, with spectacular views of the Pitons, picturesque bays and forested mountains ripe for rewarding hiking and birdwatching experiences.

Off-season rates (mid-April to mid-December) can be substantially lower than high-season rates (mid-December to mid-April). Be prepared to pay a 10 percent service charge, a government tax of 10 percent, plus a Tourism Levy of $3 or $6 (US) per person, per night, depending on whether your room rate is below or above $120.

The price categories quoted below are for a double room a night in high season, excluding tax and service.

$$$$ above US$300
$$$ US$200–300
$$ US$100–200
$ under US$100

CASTRIES

Auberge Seraphine $$ *Vielle Bay, Pointe Seraphine, Castries; tel: 758-453 2073*; www.aubergeseraphine.com. Small city hotel located close to George F.L. Charles Airport and central Castries, offering a range of simple, stylish accommodation with harbour views, an outdoor swimming pool and a handy beach shuttle.

Eudovic Guest House $ *Goodlands, Castries; tel: 758-452 2747*; eudovic@candw.lc. This small, friendly guesthouse run by local artist and woodcarver Vincent Eudovic and his family is ten minutes from the centre of Castries.

Rooms are simple and charming, with lovely furniture made from local wood, a kitchenette and fan. The artist's studio is at the same property.

Rendezvous Resort $$$$ *Malabar Beach; tel: 758-452 4211*; www.theromanticholiday.com. Couples-only, all-inclusive, medium-sized hotel set in pretty gardens with friendly staff. Cool beachfront and garden suites, spa, swimming pool and whirlpool. The beach is lovely but close to the centre of Castries and alongside George F.L. Charles Airport.

NORTH OF CASTRIES

Calabash Cove Resort & Spa $$$$ *Bonaire Estate, Marisule; tel: 758-456 3500*; www.calabashcove.com. Quiet, delightful small hotel with rooms and suites tumbling down the hillside and along the waterfront. Cottages on the water contain large, wood-panelled suites opening onto a vine-covered deck, plunge pool, outdoor shower, and hammocks; inside, you'll find every luxury going. Rooms in the main building are smaller but well appointed. Excellent food (all-inclusive packages available, but all meals are à la carte), impeccable service and lush gardens.

East Winds $$$$ *Labrelotte Bay; tel: 758-452 8212*; www.eastwinds.com. One of the Caribbean's top all-inclusives, this small and intimate 30-room beachfront hotel has lovely views of Labrelotte Bay. Stylish cottages scattered throughout the flower-filled gardens and along the beach are supremely attractive; their sunken stone-tiled showers a clear highlight. This is a long-established hotel which manages to maintain the dual feat of consistently high standards and a friendly, attentive staff. Lovely tropical gardens wrap around a gourmet restaurant, which serves up excellent grilled mahi-mahi and marlin, and a piano bar with superb wines.

Villa Beach Cottages $$$-$$$$ *Choc Bay; tel: 758-450 2884*; www.villabeachcottages.com. Self-catering cottages and suites on Choc Bay. Spacious rooms with air-conditioning; some with four poster beds, all with kitchens. Watersports facilities and outdoor pool. You can rent additional equipment from the Sandals Resort next door. The sister property, *Dauphine Estate*, at Etangs, Soufrière, offers a two-centre experience, with plantation life complementing the beach.

Windjammer Landing $$$$ *Labrelotte Bay; tel: 758-456 9000*; www.windjammer-landing.com. Sprawled over 55 hillside acres on and above Labrellotte Bay, accommodation ranges from well-appointed rooms to self-contained villas – some with private pools and chefs, all with lovely ocean views. Getting around can be a hassle since walking is not really an option; instead you're shuttled around the windy roads by minivan – celebrity guests, perhaps accustomed to being chauffeured, are not unusual. A major draw is the resort's excellent watersports outfit, as are the five onsite restaurants, three pools and gorgeous beach.

RODNEY BAY

Bay Gardens Resorts $$–$$$$ *Rodney Bay; tel: 457 8006*; www.baygardensresorts.com. There are three hotels in this locally owned group, all in Rodney Bay and popular with business and leisure travellers alike. The most luxurious is the *Bay Gardens Beach Resort*, an all-suite hotel right on Reduit Beach with spa, fitness centre, car hire, dive shop and watersports. *Bay Gardens Hotel* and the smaller *Bay Gardens Inn* are in the heart of the village, close to the road to Gros Islet. They both have comfortable rooms and a high rate of repeat visitors.

Coco Palm $$–$$$ *Rodney Bay Boulevard; tel: 758-456 2800*; www.coco-resorts.com. Stylish mid-sized hotel in the village, a great location convenient for beach, nightlife and shopping, but set back from the road to eliminate noise. Comfortable rooms and suites overlook the pool or garden; the best being on the ground floor, with French doors giving direct access to a patio and the pool.

Harmony Suites $$–$$$ *Rodney Bay; tel: 758-452 8756*; www.harmonymarinasuites.net. Comfortable, moderately priced suite accommodation near Reduit Beach with views of the marina; no children under 12. Meal plans available but there is more variety at local restaurants.

Soco House Hotel $$$ *Reduit Beach Ave, Rodney Bay; tel: 758-2851153*; www.thesocohotel.com. This adults-only boutique hotel has 76 rooms, with four price options to choose from. Staff are friendly and helpful, and there is a good on-site restaurant.

NORTH COAST

Cap Maison $$$$ *Smuggler's Cove Drive, Cap Estate; tel: 758-457 8670*; www.capmaison.com. Luxury rooms, suites and villa suites in a clifftop boutique hotel overlooking Smuggler's Cove. Spacious, comfortable, good facilities and attentive service. Panoramic views to Pigeon Point from the much-praised *Cliff at Cap* restaurant. Beach bar for daytime snacks, beach towels and watersports.

La Panache $ *Cas-en-Bas Road, Gros Islet; tel: 758-715 6910*; www.lapanache.com. Three simple, air-conditioned, self-catering apartments on a hillside, with views from the balconies over Rodney Bay and Pigeon Island. The guesthouse is clean, friendly, relaxed and quiet, with a lovely garden and swimming pool. For a two-centre holiday, the owner has another apartment in the south, between Laborie and Choiseul, overlooking a ravine with views of Gros Piton.

The bodyholiday LeSport $$$$ *Cariblue Beach, Cap Estate; tel: 758-457 7800;* www.thebodyholiday.com. A luxury, all-inclusive spa resort set on a hillside in the far north of the island with a palm-shaded beach. Suites are spacious and tastefully furnished for couples or singles. Lots of activities and sports, from archery to yoga. The restaurants serve great food and there is live entertainment. Staff are friendly and give excellent service.

MARIGOT BAY

JJ's Paradise Resort $–$$ *Marigot Bay; tel: 758-451 4761*; www.jjsparadise.com. A popular St Lucian-owned and operated resort and restaurant on a hillside close to sheltered Marigot Bay. Clean, spacious standard rooms, or air-conditioned suites and cottages with verandas overlooking the bay. Friendly and helpful staff.

Marigot Bay Resort $$$$ *Marigot Bay; tel: 758-458 5300*; www.marigotbay-resort.com. Luxury resort on the hillside running down to the waterfront, with sweeping views of the harbour and yachts, plus every amenity. Gourmet restaurants and boutique shops at The Marina Village, as well as watersports at the marina.

Marigot Beach Dive Resort $$$$ *Marigot Bay; tel: 758-451 4974*; www.marigotdiveresort.com. Ensconced on the north side of the bay, just a minute or two from the road's end by ferry, the resort's location has long been its main draw. All rooms (villas and studios) come with kitchen/ettes, and the pool, beach, watersports and shops manage to keep guests plenty busy; the open-air restaurant is named *Dolittle's* after the Rex Harrison movie filmed here in the 1960s.

Ti Kaye Village Resort $$$–$$$$ *Anse Cochon; tel: 758-456 8101*; www.tikaye.com. This remote hideaway on a cliffside south of Anse la Raye boasts romantic Caribbean-style cottages, some of which come with a private plunge pool. The beach is a short walk down and a long 169-step walk back up. Popular with honeymooners and a good choice for snorkellers and divers – the *Lesleen M* shipwreck is just offshore. The clifftop spa uses locally made, natural products.

The Villa On The Bay $$$ *Seaview Avenue, Marigot Bay; tel: 758-888 9895*; www.villa-on-the-bay.com. A stylish rental villa on the hilltop with a glorious view over the bay, run by generous and welcoming hosts who can arrange activities. Comfortable rooms have fans and verandas which catch the breeze, plus there's a pool and six decks.

SOUFRIÈRE

Anse Chastanet and Jade Mountain $$$–$$$$ *Soufrière; tel: 758-459 7000;* www.ansechastanet.com, www.jademountainstlucia.com. Stylish and spacious, with accommodation set on a hillside offering breathtaking views of the Pitons, Caribbean Sea and forest. The room to book is the luxurious suite with a missing fourth wall framing views of the majestic Pitons. The Jade Mountain suites on the hilltop are tastefully lavish, romantic and breezy, each with its own infinity pool. Superb restaurants and a lovely spa for pampering, with excellent snorkelling just offshore, and diving, mountain biking, tennis, yoga, kayaking and other activities available. The resort has a volcanic sand beach, while nearby Anse Mamin has a stretch of fine white sand.

Crystals $$$-$$$$ *Soufrière; tel: 758-384 8995*; www.stluciacrystals.com. With colourful decor and a homely vibe, five self-catering cottages offer a mix of North African and plantation-house style, with artwork scattered in every corner. Rooms all have a view of the Pitons, a plunge pool, swimming pool or whirlpool. The bar and restaurant is available for guests only, picnic lunches are available, and help with excursions offered.

Fond Doux Eco Resort $$$$ *Soufrière; tel: 758-731 3090*; www.fonddouxresort.com. Traditional chattel houses have been remodelled as comfortable guest accommodation on this working cocoa plantation. Peaceful countryside location set in tropical gardens around a French colonial estate house. Relaxing, charming, helpful staff and excellent food with ingredients from the estate.

Hummingbird Beach Resort $$ *Soufriere Bay; tel: 758-459 7232*; hbr@candw.lc. This bijou hotel (just nine rooms) is on the beach, conveniently close to town, and has a cute little pool with Piton views. The fabulous restaurant serves delicious creole food with friendly service.

La Haut Plantation $$$–$$$$ *West Coast Road, Soufrière; tel: 758-459 7008*; www.lahaut.com. A family-run guesthouse with spacious rooms and a private balcony from which to enjoy a stunning view of the Pitons. Not on the beach but it does have a fabulous infinity pool. A self-contained cottage is also available to rent. Good restaurant and great breakfasts.

Ladera Resort $$$$ *Soufrière; tel: 758-459 7323*; www.ladera.com. Upscale and exclusive hillside property of villas and suites, 3km (2 miles) from the centre of Soufrière. Rooms, crafted from local stone and rich hardwood, are open on one side with private plunge pools. Lovely tropical gardens and breathtaking views over Soufrière Bay to the Pitons; excellent cuisine at the award-winning *Dasheene Restaurant*. Spa treatments and warm mineral pools for bathing.

Rabot Hotel (Hotel Chocolat) $$$$ *Rabot Estate, Soufrière; tel: UK: +44 (0)3444 932323, US: +1-758-572-9600*; www.thehotelchocolat.com. Boutique hotel and restaurant of traditional-style wooden cottages and villas set on a working cocoa estate with glorious views of the Pitons. Clean lines with white linen and every luxury and comfort. You can take pleasant walks on the estate through fruit trees to historic battlesites, or tours of the cocoa plantation. The inviting spa offers an inventive menu of treatments, including massages using local cocoa nibs, oil and butter.

Stonefield Resort $$$$ *Soufrière; tel: 758-459 7037*; www.stonefieldresort.com. Small villa complex in beautifully landscaped gardens, almost 2km (1.2 mile) from Soufrière, and petroglyphs in the grounds. One- to three-bedroom villas are individual in style; the best have a garden shower, veranda and panoramic views of the Pitons, the sea and Soufrière. There's a swimming pool, a good restaurant and a spa which uses local products, including homegrown cocoa.

Sugar Beach $$$$ *Val des Pitons, Jalousie Bay; tel: 758-456 8000*; www.viceroyhotelsandresorts.com/sugarbeach. Luxury resort on former sugar plantation extending back from a sheltered bay wedged between the landmark Pitons. Villas are in tasteful clusters, each with a butler, every comfort and absolute privacy; white-on-white interiors adds to the chic vibe. As well as tennis, a PADI dive centre and children's activities, the rainforest spa has tree-house treatment gazebos built among the ruins of the old plantation. Delicious food is offered in the restaurants while the ultra-modern, pop-art *Cane Bar* stocks specialty rums.

Uptown Guesthouse $$ *West Coast Road, Soufrière; tel: 758-459 7437*. Warm and welcoming guesthouse peeking out from a tropical grove on the hillside. Rooms are modest but pretty, with rustic stone floors and wooden shutters accented by handpainted wall murals. The jewel in the crown here is the vista: a tantalizing glimpse of Petit Piton and Soufrière framed by private balconies and the outdoor dining terrace. The restaurant serves up good-value traditional creole cooking, served with a side of sea views. A taxi and tour service plus jeep rental also available.

VIEUX FORT AND THE SOUTH

Balenbouche Estate $$ *between Laborie and Choiseul; tel: 758-455 1244*; www.balenbouche.com. Family-run guesthouse with colonial-style self-catering cottages and villas to rent on an eighteenth-century sugar plantation that remains a working organic farm. A popular heritage site (see page 73) with tropical gardens, containing huge old trees and machinery from the sugar mill, including an old water wheel; it is used for weddings and yoga retreats. Friendly, intimate, with a rustic, faded-glory feel. Delicious home-cooked food available.

Beach House Mirage $$ *Laborie Bay, Laborie; tel: 758-455 9763.* Located right on the bay in the serene, beautiful fishing village of Laborie, this divine spot offers five comfortable rooms on the beach, all with kitchenette and terrace; the intimate beachside setting is a rarity on the island. A pristine reef not far from shore makes for excellent snorkelling. The friendly owners also have a relaxing French/creole open-air restaurant and bar on site.

Coconut Bay Resort and Spa $$$$ *Vieux Fort; tel: 758-456 9999*; www.coconutbayresortandspa.com. Currently the only resort of its kind in the south, *Coconut Bay* is a sprawling, 85-acre all-inclusive on the beach, just five minutes from the airport. Three pools, a waterpark and an activities centre will keep kids happy; tennis courts, spa and jogging trails appeal to adults; though the restaurant is not one of the island's best.

Laborie Beach House $$ *Laborie; tel: 758-455 9237*; www.laboriebeach-house.com. Offering two beachside apartments in a quiet fishing community, *Laborie Beach House* is tucked well away from any tourist hustle. Both apartments have infinity pools and kitchenettes, with good local restaurants in the village.

The Reef Beach Huts $ *Anse de Sables; tel: 758-454 3418*; www.slucia.com/reef. A few rustic wooden huts tucked behind the popular café on the beach. Ideal for windsurfers and kitesurfers who don't mind basic lodgings. Fans and mosquito nets are provided, and breakfast on the beach is included.

EAST COAST

Fox Grove Inn $ *Mon Repos, Micoud; tel: 758-455 3271*; www.foxgroveinn.com. Small country hotel close to Mamiku Gardens. The 12 simple guestrooms and self-contained apartments have en-suite showers or bathrooms and ceiling fans. Surrounded by banana and coconut plantations, with good views of Praslin Bay. There's a lovely outdoor swimming pool and an excellent restaurant on site.

INDEX

THE **MINI** ROUGH GUIDE TO

ST LUCIA

First Edition 2022

Editors: Joanna Reeves, Annie Warren, Zara Sekhavati
Author: Joanne Owen
Picture Editor: Tom Smyth
Cartography Update: Carte
Layout: Pradeep Thapliyal
Head of DTP and Pre-Press: Katie Bennett
Head of Publishing: Kate Drynan
Photography Credits: Alamy 39, 56, 64, 80; Chris Huxley/Rain Forest Adventures 46; Corbis 5T, 48, 76, 102, 107; Dreamstime 58, 74; FLPA 5M, 85; Getty Images 4MC, 4TC, 4ML, 17, 19, 21, 45, 61, 69, 70, 73, 86, 90, 102/103; iStock 1, 4TC, 4MC, 4ML, 14, 23, 26, 33, 35, 36, 40, 42, 49, 54, 59, 65, 66, 68, 72, 79, 81, 82, 89, 93, 105, 110; Mary Evans Picture Library 18; Public domain 16; Shutterstock 4TL, 5M, 6T, 6B, 7T, 7B, 10, 11, 13, 28, 31, 41, 50, 62, 71, 94, 96, 98, 100; SuperStock 78, 84
Cover Credits: Petit Piton **BlueOrange Studio/ Shutterstock**

Distribution

UK, Ireland and Europe: Apa Publications (UK) Ltd; sales@roughguides.com
United States and Canada: Ingram Publisher Services; ips@ingramcontent.com
Australia and New Zealand: Booktopia; retailer@booktopia.com.au
Worldwide: Apa Publications (UK) Ltd; sales@roughguides.com

Special Sales, Content Licensing and CoPublishing

Rough Guides can be purchased in bulk quantities at discounted prices. We can create special editions, personalised jackets and corporate imprints tailored to your needs. sales@roughguides.com; http://roughguides.com

This book was produced using **Typefi** automated publishing software.

Printed in Czech Republic

Contact us

Every effort has been made to provide accurate information in this publication, but changes are inevitable. The publisher cannot be held responsible for any resulting loss, inconvenience or injury sustained by any traveller as a result of information or advice contained in the guide. We would appreciate it if readers would call our attention to any errors or outdated information, or if you feel we've left something out. Please send your comments with the subject line "Rough Guide Mini St Lucia Update" to mail@uk.roughguides.com.